CONTENTS

D1326764

First published 2010

Elmwood Press

80 Attimore Road, Welwyn Garden City, Herts. Al8 6LP   Tel. 01707 333232

Database right Elmwood Press (maker)

ISBN 9781 906 622 190

Typeset and illustrated by Domex e-Data Pvt. Ltd. Printed and bound by Bookwell.

UNIT 1

1.1 Written calculations

1 Work out

   (a) 384×6 (b) 19×300 (c) $8.4 - 2.57$ (d) $38.02 \div 10$

   (e) $7.3 + 8$ (f) 8×463 (g) $9146 - 4839$ (h) 70×400

2 Which of the following questions gives the largest answer?

   $301 \div 7$ $240.5 \div 5$ $299.52 \div 6$

      A   B   C

3 Copy and complete this multiplication square.

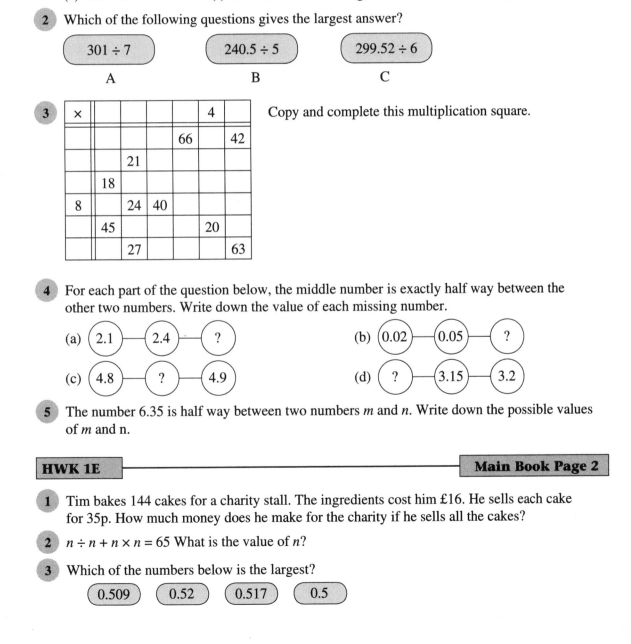

×					4	
			66		42	
	21					
18						
8		24	40			
45				20		
	27				63	

4 For each part of the question below, the middle number is exactly half way between the other two numbers. Write down the value of each missing number.

   (a) 2.1 — 2.4 — ?   (b) 0.02 — 0.05 — ?

   (c) 4.8 — ? — 4.9 (d) ? — 3.15 — 3.2

5 The number 6.35 is half way between two numbers m and n. Write down the possible values of m and n.

1 Tim bakes 144 cakes for a charity stall. The ingredients cost him £16. He sells each cake for 35p. How much money does he make for the charity if he sells all the cakes?

2 $n \div n + n \times n = 65$ What is the value of n?

3 Which of the numbers below is the largest?

   0.509 0.52 0.517 0.5

4 Natasha has an allotment. She plants 14 rows of lettuces. Each row has 14 lettuces. Neil has a slightly larger allotment and plants 15 rows each containing 15 lettuces. How many more lettuces does Neil grow than Natasha?

5 Arrange in order of size, smallest first:

(a) 0.83, 0.825, 0.814   (b) 2.6, 2.64, 2.627

6 Answer true or false:

(a) $3 + 2 \times 5 = 13$ (b) $8 \times 2 \div 4 = 4$ (c) $9 - 2 \times 3 = 21$ (d) $48 \div 8 \times 2 = 12$

7 Put each of the numbers 1, 2, 3, 4 and 5 into the boxes below to make a correct calculation.

$\square \times \square - \square \times \square = \square$

8 Zak made 160 greetings cards which cost him a total of £67.20. How much did each card cost?

HWK 2M	**Main Book Page 4**

Work out

1 6×0.6 **2** 9×0.2 **3** 16×0.2 **4** 0.8×6 **5** 0.3×0.8

6 0.2×0.6 **7** 7×0.18 **8** 0.4×0.03 **9** 0.04×0.6 **10** 0.06×12

11 0.5×17 **12** 16×0.8 **13** 3.2×0.3 **14** 0.8^2 **15** 3.2×0.3

16 0.01^2 **17** 2.6×0.02 **18** 1.2×1.2 **19** 0.8×0.11 **20** 0.1^3

HWK 2E	**Main Book Page 4**

Work out, without a calculator

1 $14 \div 0.5$ **2** $0.72 \div 0.2$ **3** $2.46 \div 0.3$ **4** $4.55 \div 0.5$ **5** $1.03 \div 0.1$

6 $0.12 \div 0.2$ **7** $0.64 \div 0.1$ **8** $0.24 \div 0.02$ **9** $0.27 \div 0.05$

10 Copy and fill in the empty boxes.

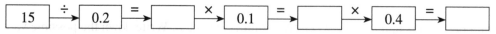

11 Copy and fill in the empty boxes.

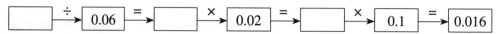

12 How many 0.15 m lengths of wood can be cut from a piece of wood which is 1.8 m long?

13 Which of the following are true or false?

(a) $16 \div 0.2 = 8$ (b) $0.7 \div 0.01 = 70$ (c) $36 \div 0.1 = 360$

(d) $0.418 \div 0.1 = 41.8$ (e) $5.2 \div 0.04 = 130$ (f) $0.169 \div 0.05 = 3.38$

14 When full, a glass contains 0.35 litres. How many glasses can be completely filled from a 2.8 litre carton of orange juice?

(a) Start in the top left box. Write down the letter 'P'.

(b) Work out the answer to the calculation in the box. Do not use a calculator.

(c) Find the answer in the top corner of another box.

(d) Write down the letter in that box.

(e) Repeat steps (b), (c) and (d) until you arrive back at the top left box. What is the message?

START ↓				
0.008	12.12	0.01	140	13.6
P	A	E	A	C
3×0.2	0.7×0.03	$0.42 \div 0.06$	5×0.03	0.3×0.2
7	0.32	50.8	430	1.32
R	I	T	E	E
$11 - 1.38$	$21 - 7.4$	$0.2 \times 0.2 \times 0.2$	$13 \div 0.5$	$0.024 \div 0.3$
26	0.06	9.62	0.6	4.33
S	E	F	R	T
$9.6 - 3.17$	$0.036 \div 0.4$	1.2×1.1	$14 \div 0.1$	0.8×0.4
0.15	0.021	0.09	0.08	6.43
C	K	M	C	P
$1.9 + 2.43$	$8.6 \div 0.02$	$4.12 + 8$	$5.08 \div 0.1$	0.02×0.5

Do not use a calculator.

Work out

1 68×37 **2** 184×46 **3** 216×29 **4** 38×528 **5** $918 \div 27$

6 $1152 \div 32$ **7** $817 \div 43$ **8** $2356 \div 62$

9 A tin of chocolates costs £5.32. How much will 12 tins cost?

10 48 pencils cost £22.08. How much does each pencil cost?

11 Work out the area of this rectangle.

128 mm

47 mm

12 There are 11 rows of chairs in a school assembly. Each row has 29 chairs. How many chairs are there in total?

13 One day a factory produces 400 clocks. The clocks are packed into boxes. What is the least number of boxes needed if one box can hold 15 clocks?

14

Shop A	**Shop B**	**Shop C**
34 packets of crisps for £14.28	41 packets of crisps for £15.99	52 packets of crisps for £21.32

Put these shops in order according to the cost of a packet of crisps, starting with the cheapest.

HWK 5M ──────────────────────────────────── **Main Book Page 8**

Answer true or false for the following questions:

1 $6 \times 0.4 < 6$ **2** $3 \times 0.2 > 3$ **3** $5 \div 0.2 > 5$ **4** $6 \div 0.1 < 6$

5 $8 \div 1.5 < 8$ **6** $4 \times 3.8 > 4$ **7** $7 \div 0.99 > 7$ **8** $10 \div 4.3 < 10$

9 $9 \div 1.1 > 9$ **10** $8 \div 0.18 > 8$ **11** $2 \div 1.9 > 2$ **12** $7 \times 0.06 < 7$

13 $9 \times 1.01 > 9$ **14** $5 \div 0.004 > 5$ **15** $3 \times 0.98 > 3$

16 Work out

(a) 2×0.06 (b) 5×0.8 (c) $4 \div 0.5$ (d) $3 \div 0.02$ (e) 9×0.9 (f) $2 \div 0.001$

17 x^2 is smaller than x. What can you say about the value of x?

18 $\frac{a}{b}$ is larger than a, what can you say about the value of b?

19 $3 \div m$ is smaller than 3. What can you say about the value of m?

20 n^2 is larger than n. What can you say about the value of n?

1.2 Using algebra

HWK 1M ──────────────────────────────────── **Main Book Page 10**

Simplify the following expressions:

1 $5y \times 3$ **2** $4x \times 9$ **3** $30a \div 6$ **4** $24p \div 8$ **5** $56m \div 7$

6 $8 \times 5y$ **7** $4 \times 9n$ **8** $27m \div 9$ **9** $p \times p$ **10** $4n \times n$

11 $y \times 5y$ **12** $8a \times 2a$ **13** $4y \times 6y$ **14** $18m \div 6$ **15** $45a \div 15$

16 $3p \times 10p$ **17** $32a \div 4$ **18** $y \times 8y$ **19** $5a \times 4b$ **20** $9p \times 6q$

21 $48p \div 6$ **22** $7m \times 9n$ **23** $15y \times 7$ **24** $6a \times 6a$

25 Answer true or false:

(a) $5n \times n = 6n$ (b) $22y \div 2 = 11y$ (c) $5 \times 7m = 35m$

(d) $42m \div 6 = 8m$ (e) $2a \times 3b = 5ab$ (f) $4a \times 4a = 8a^2$

| HWK 1E | Main Book Page 11 |

In questions **1** to **6** write down the expression you are left with after following the instructions.

1 Start with n, double it and then add 7.

2 Start with y, subtract 4 and then treble the result.

3 Start with m, multiply by 6 and then subtract the result from 37.

4 Start with p, treble it and then add q.

5 Start with n, subtract it from 14 and then multiply the result by y.

6 Start with x, treble it and add p. Multiply this result by m.

7 James has £30. He buys two magazines each costing £n. How much money does he still have left?

8 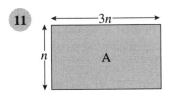 Oranges £m for 10

(a) What is the cost of one orange?

(b) What is the cost of 20 oranges?

9 Rachel weighs x kg and Simon weighs y kg. Rachel is heavier than Simon. During the next two months, Rachel puts on m kg and Simon stays at the same weight. How much more does Rachel now weigh than Simon?

10 Will has n sweets. He eats 7 sweets and gives the rest to his sister. She eats three-quarters of these sweets. How many sweets does his sister now have?

11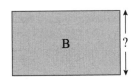

The perimeter of square B is the same as the perimeter of rectangle A.

Write down an expression for the area of square B.

12 Rosa has m cups of tea on Monday, n cups of tea on Tuesday and w cups of tea on Wednesday. Write down an expression for the mean average number of cups of tea per day for Rosa.

6

Expand (multiply out)

1 $2(3n + 4)$ **2** $5(4y - 3)$ **3** $4(2x - 5)$ **4** $6(3 + 7n)$ **5** $3(2 + 9x)$

6 $7(1 + 3y)$ **7** $4(6x - 5)$ **8** $9(2m - 7)$ **9** $8(3 + n)$ **10** $n(n + 8)$

11 $y(y - 4)$ **12** $m(3m + 2)$ **13** $4x(x - 3)$ **14** $6m(1 + m)$ **15** $3n(4n + 3)$

16 $5y(4 - 2y)$ **17** $5n(3n - 7)$ **18** $8x(5 - 3x)$

Remove the brackets and simplify.

1 $3(2x + 4) + 5$ **2** $8(2y + 7) + 10y$ **3** $4(3m + 1) + 3(5m + 3)$

4 $5(4a + 9) + 4(2a + 5)$ **5** $2(9x + 5) + 4(2x + 7)$ **6** $7(3 + 5n) + 6(3n + 1)$

7 Write down an expression for the total area of these three rectangles. Simplify your answer.

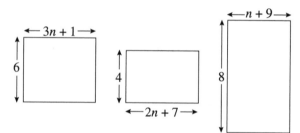

Remove the brackets and simplify.

8 $4(3n + 5) + 3(2n - 4)$ **9** $5(4a + 5) + 6(3a - 2)$ **10** $6(5x + 3) - 4(2x - 5)$

11 $7(3y + 2) - 4(4y - 7)$ **12** $8m + 4(2m + 3) - 10m$ **13** $4(6n + 5) - 2(10n + 9)$

14 $5(4x + 1) - 3(5x - 2)$ **15** $4y + 6(2y - 1) + 3$ **16** $8(n + 7) + 4(3n + 2) - 9n$

17 $5(3y + 9) - 4(y + 6) + 10$

$A = x + 4$ $B = 4x - 3$ $C = 2x + 5$ $D = 3x$

Find the value of each expression below, in terms of x. Give your answers in their simplest form.
For example: $2C + B - D = 2(2x + 5) + 4x - 3 - 3x$

$= 4x + 10 + 4x - 3 - 3x$

$= 5x + 7$

1 $A + B$ **2** $3A + C$ **3** $A + C + D$ **4** $2C - D$ **5** $2B + 3D$

6 $4A + 2C + 4D$ **7** $3A + D - C$ **8** $3C + B + 5D$ **9** $5A - B$ **10** $C + 2D - A$

11 $5C - 2D + A$ **12** $2A + B + 3C + 2D$

13 Answer 'true' or 'false'.

(a)
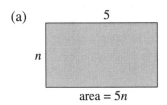
area = 5n

(b)
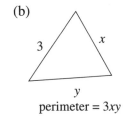
perimeter = 3xy

(c)
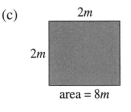
area = 8m

14 Answer 'true' or 'false'.

(a)
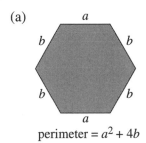
perimeter = $a^2 + 4b$

(b)
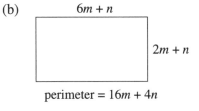
perimeter = 16m + 4n

(c)
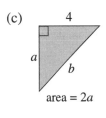
area = 2a

15 Cheryl says that $(m - n)$ is equal to $(n - m)$. Pete says she is wrong. Who is correct? Explain why you think this.

HWK 4M ──────────────────────────────── **Main Book Page 15**

Copy and complete.

1 $6x + 8 = 2(3x + \square)$

2 $9y - 15 = 3(3y - \square)$

3 $12a - 15 = 3(\square - \square)$

4 $14m + 21 = \square(2m + \square)$

5 $10n - 30 = \square(\square - \square)$

6 $32p - 20 = \square(\square - 5)$

Factorise the following expressions.

7 $7x + 28$
8 $18a + 20$
9 $22y - 55$
10 $10p + 16$

11 $15x - 35y$
12 $6m - 14n$
13 $21a + 49b$
14 $20m + 45n$

15 $6x + 12y + 15z$
16 $8m + 18n + 6p$
17 $9a + 21b - 12c$
18 $15p + 45q - 10r$

19 $20x - 16y + 24z$
20 $8m - 2n - 8p$
21 $30a + 18b - 36c$

HWK 4E ──────────────────────────────── **Main Book Page 15**

Copy and complete.

1 $bc - by = b(c - \square)$

2 $n^2 + 8n = n(\square + 8)$

3 $6a^2 + 4a = 2a(\square + 2)$

4 $10x^2 - xy = x(\square - \square)$

5 $mn + 7m^2 = m(\square + \square)$

6 $3a^2 + 6ab = \square(a + 2b)$

8

Factorise the following expressions.

7 $x^2 + 5x$ **8** $9y^2 + 7y$ **9** $a - 3a^2$ **10** $9n^2 + 3n$ **11** $ab - a^2$

12 $8x^2 - 12x$ **13** $16a^2 - 12ab$ **14** $20n^2 + 6n$ **15** $10xy + 5xyz$ **16** $6mnp - 8mn$

17 $5x^2 + 8xy$ **18** $14ab - 21abc$ **19** $3p^2 + 12pqr$ **20** $n^3 + mn$ **21** $x^3 + x$

1.3 Geometrical reasoning

HWK 1M ─────────────────────────── **Main Book Page 19**

1 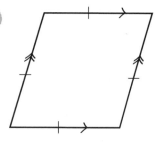 Name this shape,

2 Which shape has more lines of symmetry — a rectangle or a parallelogram?

3 Copy this diagram. Join the points and complete the shape to make a trapezium.

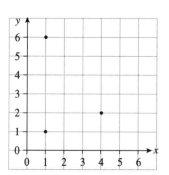

4 Answer 'true' or 'false':
'The diagonals of a parallelogram are equal in length'.

5 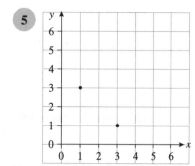 Copy this diagram,
Using the two points shown as vertices (corners) of a kite, complete a drawing of the kite.

6 In which of the following shapes are the diagonals perpendicular to each other?

(square) (rectangle) (kite) (rhombus) (parallelogram) (trapezium)

HWK 1E ━━━━━━━━━━━━━━━━━━━━━━━━━━━━━ **Main Book Page 20**

Find the angles marked with letters.

1
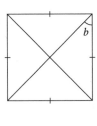
101°
87°
a
65°

2
b

3
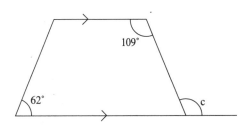
109°
62°
c

4
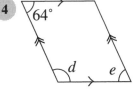
64°
d   e

5
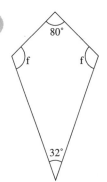
80°
f   f
32°

6
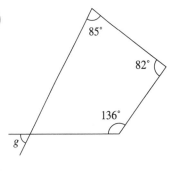
85°
82°
136°
g

7
115°
h

8
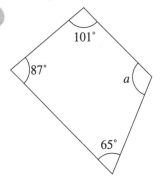
i
i
i
72°

9
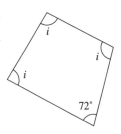
j
4j
4j
j

HWK 2M ━━━━━━━━━━━━━━━━━━━━━━━━━━━━━ **Main Book Page 22**

1 What is the name of a regular polygon with 8 sides?

2 How many lines of symmetry has a regular hexagon?

3 Name this shape.

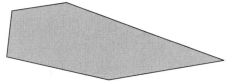

4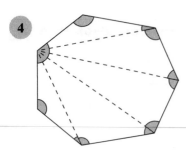

The angles in each triangle add up to 180°.
What do all the angles in this polygon add up to?

5 What do all the angles in this polygon add up to?

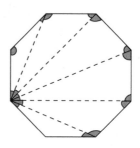

6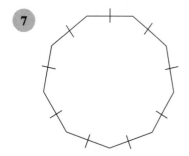

Interior angle

(a) What do all the angles in this polygon add up to?

(b) What is the size of angle x if all the interior angles are equal?

7

All the angles are equal inside this regular nonagon (9 sides).

What is the size of one interior angle?

HWK 2E ——————————————— **Main Book Page 23**

Remember: for a polygon with n sides:
  sum of interior angles $= (n - 2) \times 180°$

1 Find the value of $(n - 2) \times 180°$ when $n = 14$.

2 Find the sum of the angles in a polygon with

   (a) 12 sides   (b) 16 sides   (c) 20 sides

3 Find the sum of all the angles in this polygon with 8 sides then find the value of angle *x*.

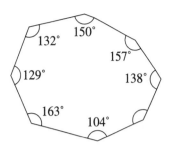

4 All the angles in a regular polygon are equal. Find the sum of all the angles in a regular decagon (10 sides) then find the size of one interior angle.

5 Find the angles marked with letters.

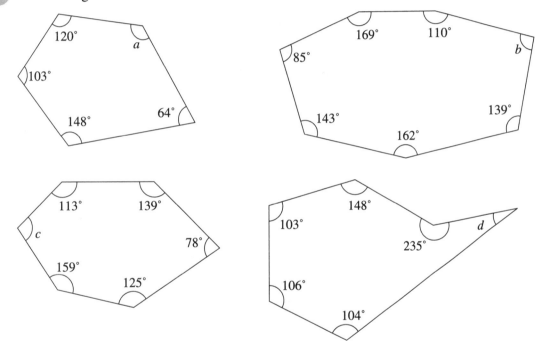

HWK 3M
Main Book Page 24

Remember: the sum of the exterior angles of a
polygon is 360°

1 Find the size of each exterior angle of a regular octagon.

2 (a) Calculate the size of each exterior angle for a regular pentagon.

   (b) Find the size of each interior angle for a regular pentagon.

3 (a) Find the exterior angles of regular polygons with (i) 20 sides (ii) 30 sides

   (b) Find the interior angle of the above polygons.

12

4 The diagram shows some of the interior angles of a regular polygon.

(a) Write down the size of an exterior angle for this polygon.

(b) How many sides has this polygon?

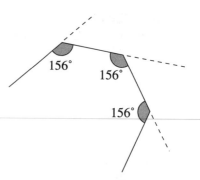

156°   156°

156°

5 Each exterior angle of a regular polygon is 40°. How many sides has the polygon?

6

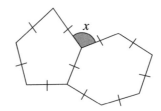

101°

107°

a   43°

36°   b

c

Find the values of angles *a*, *b* and *c*.

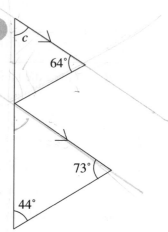

x

7 A regular pentagon is attached to a regular hexagon as shown. Find the value of angle *x*.

HWK 3E ─────────────────────────────── **Main Book Page 25**

Find the angles marked with letters.

1

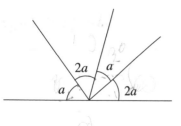

2a   a

a   2a

2

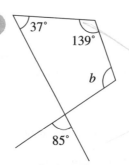

37°
139°

b

85°

3

c

64°

73°

44°

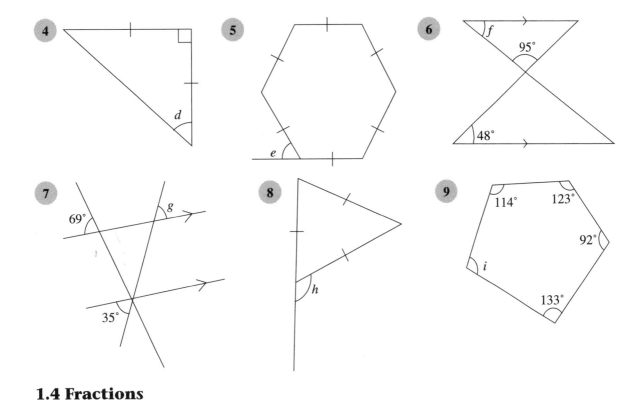

1.4 Fractions

HWK 1M ——————————————————————— **Main Book Page 27**

1 Work out the following. Cancel answers when necessary.

(a) $\frac{2}{3} \times \frac{9}{11}$ (b) $\frac{4}{7} \times \frac{3}{8}$ (c) $\frac{4}{5} \times \frac{15}{16}$ (d) $\frac{5}{6} \times \frac{9}{20}$

(e) $\frac{7}{10} \times \frac{6}{7}$ (f) $\frac{11}{15} \times \frac{10}{13}$ (g) $\frac{4}{9} \times \frac{2}{3}$ (h) $\frac{3}{7} \times \frac{21}{25}$

2

The area of shape Q is 54 cm². The area of shape P is $\frac{5}{9}$ of the area of shape Q.

Find the area of shape P.

3 Harry has £48. He spends two-thirds of the money on a shirt. He spends five-eigths of the remaining money on some food. How much money does he have left?

4 Work out the following, Cancel answers when necessary.

(a) $\frac{2}{3} \div \frac{3}{4}$ (b) $\frac{5}{6} \div \frac{8}{9}$ (c) $\frac{2}{9} \div \frac{5}{6}$ (d) $\frac{9}{14} \div \frac{9}{10}$

(e) $\frac{7}{10} \div \frac{4}{5}$ (f) $\frac{3}{5} \div \frac{2}{3}$ (g) $\frac{6}{11} \div \frac{25}{33}$ (h) $\frac{3}{4} \div \frac{11}{12}$

5 Maisie has 60 sweets. She gives $\frac{3}{5}$ of the sweets to her brother and eats the rest. Her brother eats $\frac{2}{3}$ of his share of the sweets. Who eats the most sweets?

HWK 1E ————————————————————————————— **Main Book Page 28**

1 Answer true or false.

(a) $1\frac{1}{4} \times \frac{3}{10} = \frac{5}{4} \times \frac{3}{10} = \frac{15}{40} = \frac{3}{8}$

(b) $2\frac{1}{2} \times \frac{2}{5} = \frac{5}{2} \times \frac{2}{5} = \frac{25}{10} \times \frac{4}{10} = \frac{100}{10} = \frac{10}{1}$

2 Work out

(a) $3\frac{1}{2} \times \frac{4}{9}$ (b) $1\frac{3}{4} \times 1\frac{1}{3}$ (c) $3\frac{1}{4} \times 1\frac{3}{5}$ (d) $2\frac{2}{3} \times \frac{6}{7}$ (e) $5\frac{1}{2} \times 1\frac{3}{5}$ (f) $1\frac{5}{6} \times 1\frac{1}{2}$

3 Copy and complete:

$2\frac{4}{5} \div \frac{3}{5} = \frac{\square}{5} \div \frac{3}{10} = \frac{\square}{\cancel{5}_1} \times \frac{\cancel{10}^{\,2}}{\square} = \frac{\square}{\square} = 9\frac{\square}{\square}$

4 Work out

(a) $2\frac{1}{4} \div \frac{3}{5}$ (b) $1\frac{3}{4} \div 1\frac{1}{2}$ (c) $2\frac{1}{3} \div 1\frac{5}{6}$

5 Which gives the odd answer out?

$\left(1\frac{2}{3} \times \frac{5}{1}\right)$ $\left(1\frac{2}{3} \times \frac{1}{5}\right)$ $\left(1\frac{2}{3} \times 5\right)$

A B C

HWK 2M ————————————————————————————— **Main Book Page 29**

1 Work out the following. Cancel answers when necessary.

(a) $\frac{1}{3} + \frac{2}{5}$ (b) $\frac{3}{7} + \frac{2}{9}$ (c) $\frac{2}{3} - \frac{1}{4}$ (d) $\frac{4}{5} - \frac{2}{7}$

(e) $\frac{1}{4} - \frac{1}{5}$ (f) $\frac{3}{7} + \frac{1}{8}$ (g) $\frac{7}{10} - \frac{2}{3}$ (h) $\frac{8}{9} - \frac{1}{2}$

(i) $\frac{9}{10} - \frac{7}{8}$ (j) $\frac{3}{11} + \frac{2}{5}$ (k) $\frac{5}{9} + \frac{3}{20}$ (l) $\frac{19}{20} - \frac{4}{5}$

(m) $\frac{3}{4} - \frac{5}{12}$ (n) $\frac{4}{7} + \frac{1}{15}$ (o) $\frac{2}{9} + \frac{7}{12}$ (p) $\frac{11}{12} - \frac{3}{8}$

2 There are loads of identical pizzas at a party.

Dave ate $\frac{1}{3}$ of a pizza and $\frac{4}{9}$ of another pizza.

Simone ate $\frac{2}{9}$ of a pizza then $\frac{1}{3}$ of another and then $\frac{2}{5}$ of another.

Sinan ate $\frac{2}{3}$ of a pizza and $\frac{7}{15}$ of another.

Who ate the most pizza?

> Remember: $3\frac{2}{3} = \frac{3 \times 3 + 2}{3} = \frac{11}{3}$ $\frac{18}{5} = 18 \div 5 = 3\frac{3}{5}$

1 Change the following fractions into improper fractions.

(a) $4\frac{2}{5}$ (b) $3\frac{3}{4}$ (c) $7\frac{1}{2}$ (d) $1\frac{7}{8}$

2 Copy and complete:

$$3\frac{1}{2} - 1\frac{2}{3} = \frac{\Box}{2} - \frac{\Box}{3} = \frac{\Box - \Box}{6} = \frac{\Box}{6} = \Box\frac{\Box}{6}$$

3 Work out

(a) $2\frac{3}{4} - \frac{8}{9}$ (b) $2\frac{1}{2} + \frac{3}{5}$ (c) $5\frac{1}{3} - \frac{7}{8}$

(d) $1\frac{2}{3} + 1\frac{3}{4}$ (e) $3\frac{1}{4} - 1\frac{1}{6}$ (f) $4\frac{2}{3} - 2\frac{5}{8}$

4 An audio book comes on 3 CD's. CD1 runs for $1\frac{1}{3}$ hours. CD2 runs for $2\frac{1}{4}$ hours and CD3 runs for $1\frac{4}{5}$ hours.

What is the total time length of the audio book?

5 Work out $3\frac{2}{5} + 2\frac{3}{4} - 4\frac{9}{10}$

1.5 Scatter graphs

1 Match one statement to each scatter graph to describe the correlation.

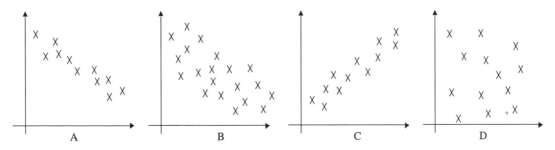

1	strong positive correlation	2	strong negative correlation
3	weak positive correlation	4	weak negative correlation
5	no correlation		

16

2 The table below shows the heights and weights of 10 young people.

weight (kg)	60	80	60	40	80	60	48	72	50	78
height (m)	1.6	1.62	1.71	1.5	1.8	1.52	1.62	1.56	1.46	1.74

(a) Plot this information on a scatter graph.

(b) Describe the correlation between the weight and height of these people.

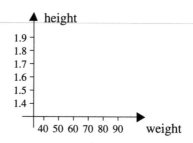

1

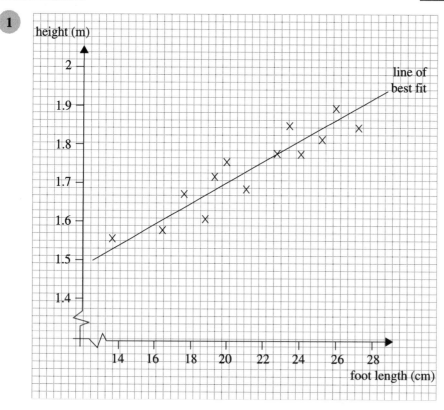

This scatter graph shows the heights of some people and their corresponding foot lengths.

(a) Describe the correlation.

(b) Estimate the height of a person with a foot length of 14 cm.

(c) Estimate the foot length of a person of height 1.76 m.

2 The table below shows the marks obtained by some students in a calculator and a non-calculator maths test.

calculator	54	70	86	60	90	50	76	40	96	66	80
non-calculator	50	60	80	70	72	60	70	54	78	54	76

(a) Plot this data on a scatter graph, with the calculator marks on the horizontal axis.

(b) Draw the line of best fit.

(c) Estimate the non-calculator mark of a student who got 56 in the calculator test.

(d) Estimate the calculator mark of a student who got 76 in the non-calculator test.

3 The table below shows the daily hours of sunshine and the daily amount of rainfall over a two week period for a Pacific island.

sunshine (h)	10	5.5	7.5	16	6	1	11	12	2	4	12.5	1	13	9
rainfall (mm)	14	26	21	10	21	34	20	14	26	30	10	29	15	17

(a) Plot this data on a scatter graph, with the hours of sunshine on the horizontal axis.

(b) Estimate the hours of rainfall on a day when there are 8 hours of sunshine.

1.6 Index laws

HWK 1M	Main Book Page 35

1 Which is the largest? 2^3 or 3^2 or 7

2 Answer true or false:

(a) $5^3 = 5 \times 3$ (b) $2^4 = 2 \times 2 \times 2 \times 2$

(c) $4^3 = 4 \times 4 \times 4$ (d) $7^3 = 3 \times 3 \times 3 \times 3 \times 3 \times 3 \times 3$

3 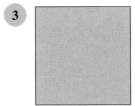 Work out the area of this square.

← 16 cm →

4 $5^4 = 5 \times 5 \times 5 \times 5$ (5^4 is called 'index form')
Write in index form

(a) $6 \times 6 \times 6$ (b) $9 \times 9 \times 9 \times 9 \times 9$ (c) $4 \times 4 \times 4 \times 4 \times 4 \times 4$

(d) 10×10 (e) $8 \times 8 \times 8 \times 8$ (f) $2 \times 2 \times 2 \times 2 \times 2 \times 2 \times 2 \times 2$

(g) $a \times a \times a \times a$ (h) $m \times m \times m$ (i) $n \times n \times n \times n \times n \times n \times n$

18

5 Work out the following:

(a) $3^2 - 1^3$ (b) $2^5 - 4^2$ (c) $10^3 - 5^3$

(d) $4^3 - 8^2$ (e) $11^2 + 3^4$ (f) $1^3 + 2^3 + 3^3 + 4^3$

| **HWK 1E** | **Main Book Page 36** |

1 Work out without a calculator:

(a) $\sqrt{49}$ (b) $\sqrt{64}$ (c) $\sqrt{9} - \sqrt{4}$

(d) $\sqrt{81} + \sqrt{25}$ (e) $\sqrt{121} - \sqrt{100}$ (f) $\sqrt{1} + \sqrt{16} + \sqrt{144}$

2 Find the missing numbers:

(a) $3^{\square} = 81$ (b) $\square^4 = 16$ (c) $\square^3 = 1000$

(d) $\square^4 = 0$ (e) $\sqrt{\square} = 6$ (f) $\sqrt{\square} = 20$

3

area = 81 cm^2

Find the perimeter of this square.

4 Use a calculator to find the following, correct to one decimal place.

(a) $\sqrt{56}$ (b) $\sqrt[3]{216}$ (c) $\sqrt[3]{50}$ (d) $\sqrt{1.69}$

5 Square A has an area of 6.25 cm². Each side in square B is three times longer than each side in square A. Find the area of square B.

6 The volume of this cube is 343000 cm³.
Find the area of the shaded face shown.

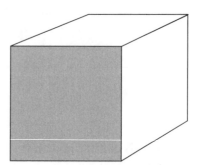

7 Use a calculator to work out the following:

$$\sqrt[3]{13824} + 13^2 - \sqrt{289} - \sqrt[3]{6859}$$

1 Simplify

(a) $m^8 \div m^5$ 　　(b) $p^7 \div p^3$ 　　(c) $n^4 \times n^3$ 　　(d) $x^{10} \div x^2$ 　　(e) $y^4 \times y^4$ 　　(f) $m^3 \times m$

2 Answer true or false:

(a) $4^2 \times 4^3 = 4^6$ 　　　　(b) $2^8 \div 2^3 = 2^5$ 　　　　(c) $5^{10} \div 5^5 = 5^2$

(d) $8^4 \div 8^3 = 8$ 　　　　(e) $9^{12} \div 9 = 9^{11}$ 　　　　(f) $6^8 \div 6^4 = 6^4$

3 Write down the value of:

(a) 3^0 　　　　(b) $7^4 \div 7^2$ 　　　　(c) 5^0 　　　　(d) $3^7 \div 3^6$

4 Work out and write each answer in index form.

(a) $\dfrac{6^4 \times 6^3}{6^5}$ 　　　　(b) $\dfrac{5^4 \times 5^6}{5^3}$ 　　　　(c) $\dfrac{2^5 \times 2^3 \times 2^2}{2^4 \times 2^4}$

(d) $\dfrac{m^6 \times m^3}{m^4}$ 　　　　(e) $\dfrac{n^5 \times n^3 \times n^6}{n^7 \times n^2}$ 　　　　(f) $\dfrac{m^{10}}{m^3 \times m}$

5 Which is the larger answer and by how much?

$$\boxed{\dfrac{2^4 \times 2^5}{2^6}} \quad \text{or} \quad \boxed{\dfrac{2^3 \times 2^7 \times 2^4}{2^6 \times 2^6}}$$
　　　P　　　　　　　　　Q

6 $\dfrac{3^7 \times \square \times 3^4}{3^8} = 3^7$ 　　　Write down the number which belongs in the empty box.

1 Simplify

(a) $(m^3)^4$ 　　　　(b) $(y^5)^2$ 　　　　(c) $(n^6)^4$

2 Answer true or false:

(a) $(5^2)^3 = 5^5$ 　　　　(b) $(3^4)^2 = 3^8$ 　　　　(c) $(2^3)^2 \times 2^2 = 2^8$

(d) $(4^2)^4 = 4^6$ 　　　　(e) $(7^3)^5 \div 7^{10} = 7^5$ 　　　　(f) $(9^2)^2 \times (9^3)^2 = 9^{24}$

3 Work out and write each answer in index form.

(a) $\dfrac{(7^4)^3}{7^8}$ 　　(b) $\dfrac{(3^5)^3}{3^{10}}$ 　　(c) $(2^6)^3 \times 2^3$ 　　(d) $\dfrac{9^{12}}{(9^3)^2}$ 　　(e) $(4^4)^5 \times (4^3)^3$

(f) $\dfrac{(m^3)^4}{(m^2)^5}$ 　　(g) $\dfrac{(n^4)^5 \times n^7}{n^{16}}$ 　　(h) $\dfrac{m^6 \times (m^3)^3}{(m^2)^6}$ 　　(i) $\dfrac{(n^4)^4 \times (n^2)^6}{(n^5)^5}$

20

4 Give each final answer as an ordinary number.

(a) $3 \times (3^2)^2$

(b) $\dfrac{(5^2)^6 \times 5^4}{(5^5)^3}$

(c) $\dfrac{(7^4)^3}{(7^2)^5}$

(d) $\dfrac{6^4 \times 6^6}{(6^4)^2}$

(e) $\dfrac{(2^3)^3 \times (2^4)^2}{(2^7)^2}$

(f) $\dfrac{(4^3)^6}{(4^4)^3 \times (4^2)^2}$

5 Simplify

$$\dfrac{(3^5)^4 \times (3^2)^3 \times 3^9}{(3^2)^7 \times 3^5 \times (3^4)^2}$$

UNIT 2

2.1 Using a calculator

Use a calculator to work out each answer correct to 2 decimal places.

1 $5.312 + \frac{2.4}{3.7}$

2 $\frac{5.18 + 0.196}{2.09}$

3 $\frac{4.317 - 1.096}{2.68 \times 0.34}$

4 $0.73 + (0.169 \times 2.3)$

5 $\frac{5.7}{2.3} + 3.182$

6 $\frac{3.2}{1.916} + \frac{2.17}{4.4}$

7 $\frac{1.13 \times 2.77}{4.49 + 3.16}$

8 $\frac{(1.7 - 0.29)^2}{3.08}$

9 $\frac{1.47}{3.6} + 3.14^2$

10 Work out the answers and place each question below in order of size, starting with the smallest:

$$\frac{7.14^2 - 6.39}{1.04}$$

A

$$\frac{5.173 + 2.53}{0.012}$$

B

$$\frac{1.93 \times 2.07}{5.17 \times 3.16}$$

C

11 A machine cuts 12 rectangular pieces of card every minute.
Find the exact total area of card that the machine cuts in one hour.

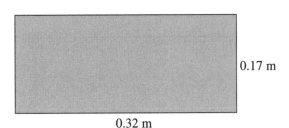

0.17 m

0.32 m

12 Calculate to one decimal place:

$$\frac{3.6 + 2.14^2}{5.07 - 1.89} + \frac{2.178}{0.67^2}$$

Use a calculator to work out each answer correct to 2 decimal places.

1 3.9^4

2 $2.4^3 + 4.2^3$

3 $5.18^3 - 7.4^2$

4 $(9.14 - 2.77)^3$

5 $384 - 3.3^4$

6 $1.6^5 + 2.2^6$

7 $\frac{1}{9} - \frac{1}{11}$

8 $\frac{4}{5}$ of $\left(\frac{2}{3}\right)^2$

9 $\left(\frac{3}{4}\right)^2 + \left(\frac{1}{3}\right)^3$

10

ham £6.80/kg
bread roll 38p each
apples £2.70 for 10
cheese £5.30/kg

(a) Calculate the cost of 4 bread rolls, 3 apples, $\frac{1}{2}$ kg of cheese and $\frac{1}{4}$ kg of ham.

(b) How much change from £10 will Jennie get if she buys 0.4 kg of ham, 7 apples, 0.3 kg of cheese and 6 bread rolls?

11 Work out each answer correct to 2 decimal places.

(a) $2.146 + \sqrt{10.14}$

(b) $\sqrt{\dfrac{6.3 - 1.119}{8.2 + 1.314}}$

(c) $\sqrt{\dfrac{2.18^2}{0.07}}$

(d) $2.8^5 - \sqrt{\dfrac{2.6}{0.93}}$

(e) $\sqrt{\dfrac{18.65}{\sqrt{5.27} + \sqrt{1.19}}}$

(f) $\frac{3}{8} \times \sqrt{7.6}$

12 Calculate the exact perimeter of this square.

area
= 13.9876 m²

2.2 Circles

HWK 1M ———————————————————————————— **Main Book Page 57**

Give each answer correct to 1 decimal place in this Exercise.

1 Which circle has the larger circumference and by how much?

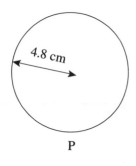

4.8 cm

P

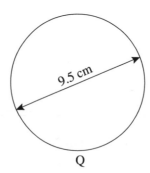

9.5 cm

Q

2 The distance from the centre of a planet to its surface is 1592 miles. Find the circumference of the planet.

3 A pram wheel has diameter 12 cm. Stuart takes his child in the pram for a walk. During the walk each pram wheel makes 1375 complete rotations. How far does Stuart walk? Give your answer in metres.

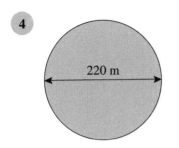

4 Kate runs once around a circular
lake of diameter 220 m.
Nick runs once around a
square field with each side
equal to 220 m.
How much further does
Nick run than Kate?

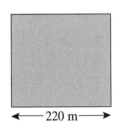

←— 220 m —→

5 The wheels on an old car have a radius of 24 cm. The car breaks down and has to be
pushed 8 m into a safe place. Calculate how many times the wheels go round completely
when the car is pushed.

| **HWK 1E** | **Main Book Page 58** |

Calculate the perimeter of each shape. All arcs are either semi-circles or quarter circles.

Give answers correct to 1 decimal place.

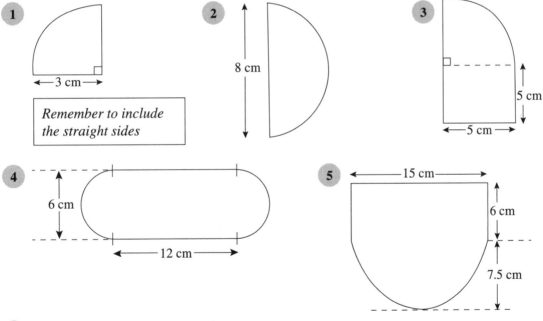

1

←— 3 cm —→

*Remember to include
the straight sides*

2

8 cm

3

5 cm

←— 5 cm —→

4

6 cm

←— 12 cm —→

5

←——— 15 cm ———→

6 cm

7.5 cm

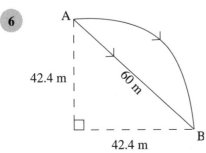

6

A

42.4 m

60 m

42.4 m

B

Anwar walks along the curved arc AB,
Kate walks directly from A to B.
How much further than Kate does Anwar walk?

7 Sadie cuts out the shaded shape shown opposite.

Calculate the perimeter of this shaded shape.

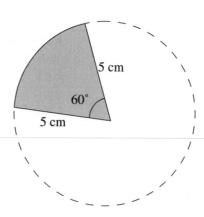

5 cm

60°

5 cm

HWK 2M ——————————————————— **Main Book Page 60**

In this Exercise give each answer correct to 1 decimal place.

1 Which circle has the larger area and by how much?

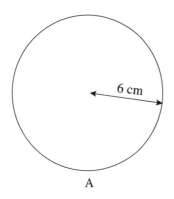

6 cm

A

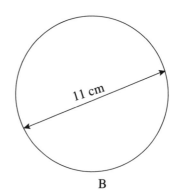

11 cm

B

2 Find the area of a circular clock of diameter 17 cm.

3 Put these shapes in order of area size, starting with the smallest.

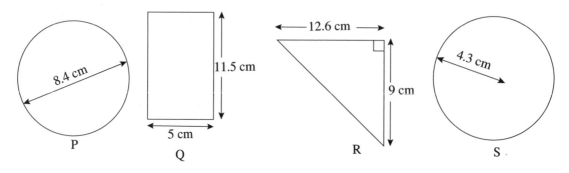

8.4 cm

P

11.5 cm

5 cm

Q

12.6 cm

9 cm

R

4.3 cm

S

In questions ④ to ⑦ find the area of each shape. All arcs are either semi-circles or quarter circles and the units are cm.

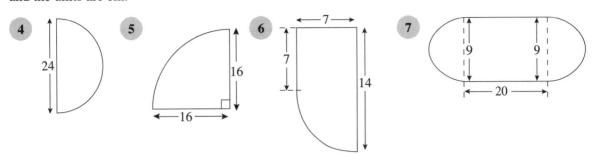

④ 24

⑤ 16, 16

⑥ 7, 7, 14

⑦ 9, 9, 20

| HWK 2E | | Main Book Page 61 |

In this exercise give each answer correct to 1 decimal place.

Find each shaded area in questions ① to ⑥. All lengths are in cm.

① 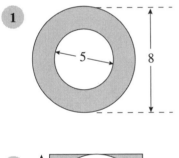 5, 8

② 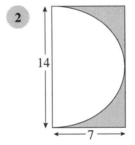 14, 7

③ 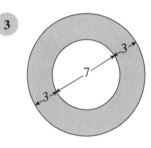 3, 7, 3

④ 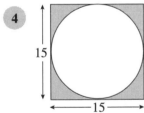 15, 15

⑤ 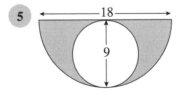 18, 9

⑥ 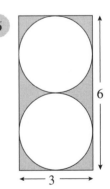 6, 3

⑦ 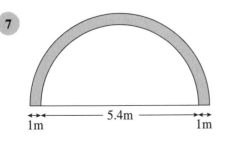 5.4m, 1m, 1m

The two arcs shown are both semi-circles. Calculate the shaded area correct to two decimal places.

2.3 Construction and scale drawing

Use only a pencil, a straight edge and a pair of compasses.

1   Draw an angle of about 70°. Construct the bisector of the angle.

2   Draw an angle of about 120°. Construct the bisector of the angle.

3   Draw a horizontal line AB of length 8 cm. Construct the perpendicular bisector of AB.

4

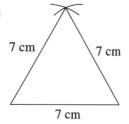

Construct an equilateral triangle of side length 7 cm.

5   Construct any equilateral triangle then bisect any angle in this triangle.
Use a protractor to check that you then have a 30° angle.

6   (a)   Construct the triangle shown opposite.

     (b)   Bisect angle ABC using ruler and compasses only.

     (c)   Measure the angle you have just constructed.

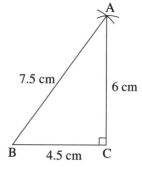

7

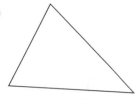

Draw any triangle. For each side of the triangle, construct the perpendicular bisectors

What do you notice about these three perpendicular bisectors?

8   Carys walks 8 km north then 3 km due west.
Construct a diagram then find out how far
Carys is from her starting position A
(ie. What is the direct distance from A to C?)

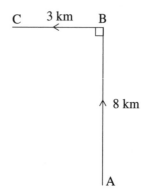

2.4 Solving equations

| **HWK 1M** | **Main Book Page 66** |

Solve the equations

1 $8x + 5 = 37$ **2** $5x - 3 = 2$ **3** $6x - 7 = 5$

4 $25 = 5x - 15$ **5** $39 = 4x + 3$ **6** $7x + 12 = 47$

7 $8x - 23 = 57$ **8** $27 = 6x + 9$ **9** $3 = 4x - 21$

Now solve these equations

10 $5 + 6x = 23$ **11** $14 = 2x - 10$ **12** $47 = 7 + 5x$

13 $41 = 4x - 19$ **14** $8x + 7 = 23$ **15** $4x - 48 = 32$

16 $74 = 2 + 8x$ **17** $5x - 64 = 26$ **18** $165 = 10x - 85$

| **HWK 1E** | **Main Book Page 66** |

Solve the equations

1 $3x + 7 = 8$ **2** $5x + 6 = 8$ **3** $9 = 4x + 3$

4 $21 = 10x - 4$ **5** $2x - 5 = 12$ **6** $x + 12 = 10$

7 $3x + 6 = 0$ **8** $4 = 3 + 5x$ **9** $1 = 13 + 6x$

Now solve these equations

10 $20 + 3x = 2$ **11** $2 = 7x - 4$ **12** $12 = 4x + 9$

13 $8x - 3 = 4$ **14** $40 + 7x = 12$ **15** $8 + 9x = 9$

16 $6x + 15 = 9$ **17** $2 = 4x + 18$ **18** $2 = 10x - 7$

| **HWK 2M** | **Main Book Page 67** |

Solve the equations

1 $5x + 3 = 2x + 21$ **2** $9x - 4 = 7x + 18$ **3** $6x - 7 = 2x + 25$

4 $7x = 3x + 20$ **5** $6x + 19 = 33 + 4x$ **6** $10x - 42 = 4x$

7 $9x - 22 = 7x + 12$ **8** $13 + 6x = x + 58$ **9** $12x - 27 = 9x$

Now solve these equations

10 $13x - 6 = 5x + 10$

11 $7x + 3 = 4x + 36$

12 $5x = 56 - 2x$

13 $9x + 28 = 3x + 82$

14 $44 + 5x = 9x$

15 $26 + 7x = 4x + 47$

16 $12x + 48 = 16x$

17 $16 - 2x = 11 + 3x$

18 $29 + 5x = 56 - 4x$

HWK 2E
Main Book Page 67

Solve the equations

1 $7x + 13 = 2x + 3$

2 $6x + 18 = 6 + 3x$

3 $9x - 4 = 2x + 1$

4 $4x - 8 = 3x + 2$

5 $7x + 16 = 5x + 19$

6 $4x + 17 = x + 8$

7 $11x + 7 = 8x - 5$

8 $9x - 12 = 4x + 18$

9 $2x - 8 = 3x + 23$

10 Manchester united have $(4n - 2)$ points and Chelsea have $(2n + 14)$ points.
How many points does each team have if they have the same number of points?

Now solve these equations.

11 $17 + 6x = 3x + 2$

12 $5x + 16 = 4x + 1$

13 $8x - 14 = 4x + 4$

14 $2 - 9x = 10 - 5x$

15 $4 + 11x = 10 - x$

16 $8 - 2x = 8 + 4x$

HWK 3M
Main Book Page 68

1 Copy and complete:

(a) $3(x + 7) = 33$

$\boxed{} + 21 = 33$

$\boxed{} = 12$

$x = \boxed{}$

(b) $4(3x - 2) = 52$

$12x - \boxed{} = 52$

$12x = \boxed{}$

$x = \boxed{}$

Solve these equations

2 $5(4x + 1) = 85$

3 $6(2x - 5) = 18$

4 $8(3x + 2) = 40$

5 $2(7x + 1) = 100$

6 $3(3x - 6) = 90$

7 $9(4x - 7) = 45$

8 $4(6x - 25) = 140$

9 $10(4x + 3) = 110$

10 $7(2x - 12) = 140$

Now solve these equations

11 $70 = 5(2x - 4)$

12 $99 = 9(4x - 5)$

13 $12(x + 3) = 180$

14 $8x = 2(3x + 6)$

15 $3(4x - 1) = 8$

16 $48 = 6(3 + x)$

HWK 3E ──────────────────────────── **Main Book Page 69**

Solve the equations

1 $3(3x + 4) = 8(2x - 2)$

2 $2(5x + 3) = 13(3x - 4)$

3 $4(3x - 2) = 8(x + 2)$

4 $7(4x + 1) = 13(3x - 2)$

5 $5(6x - 7) = 1 + 12x$

6 $10(2x - 3) = 7(x + 5)$

Now solve these equations

7 $6(5x - 4) = 31(x - 1)$

8 $4(7x + 2) = 38(1 + x)$

9 $3(x + 6) = 2(2x + 11)$

10 $5(2x + 5) = 7(7 + 2x)$

11 $3(6x - 1) = 8x + 4$

12 $2(3 + 4x) = 3(2x + 5)$

HWK 4M ──────────────────────────── **Main Book Page 70**

In questions **1** to **5** I am thinking of a number. Use the information to form an equation and then solve it to find the number.

1 If we multiply the number by 4 and then subtract 13, the answer is 15.

2 If we multiply the number by 6 and then subtract 4, the answer we get is the same as when we treble the number and add 8.

3 If we multiply the number by 5 and then add 15, the answer we get is the same as when we double the number and add 36.

4 If we treble the number, the answer we get is the same as when we double the number and add 24.

5 If we multiply the number by 7 and then subtract 9, we get the same answer as when we treble the number and add 11.

6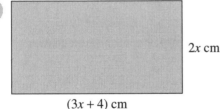

(a) Find x if the perimeter is 78 cm.

(b) Find the actual area of the rectangle.

$2x$ cm

$(3x + 4)$ cm

7 The length of a rectangle is 9 more than its width. If the perimeter of the rectangle is 110 cm, find its width. [Hint: Let the width be x cm]

8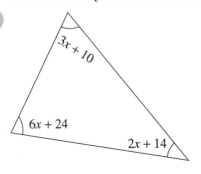

Use the angles in this triangle to form an equation involving x and solve it to find x.

$3x + 10$

$6x + 24$

$2x + 14$

9 The opposite sides in a parallelogram are equal.

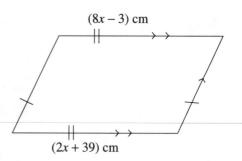

$(8x - 3)$ cm

(a) Write down an equation involving x.

(b) Solve the equation to find x.

(c) Write down the actual length of the top side of the parallelogram.

$(2x + 39)$ cm

10

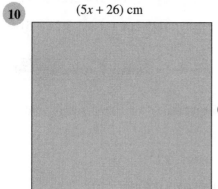

$(5x + 26)$ cm

$(10x - 4)$ cm

The diagram shows a square. Find the length of each side of the square and hence find the area of the square.

HWK 4E ———————————————————— **Main Book Page 71**

In questions **1** to **5** I am thinking of a number. Use the information to form an equation and then solve it to find the number.

1 If I treble the number, subtract 1 and then treble the result, the answer is 42.

2 If I add 8 to the number and then multiply the result by 6, I get the same answer as when I add 58 to the number.

3 If I subtract 3 from the number and then multiply the result by 4, I get the same answer as when I add 1 to the number and then double the result.

4 If I multiply the number by 5 and add 6, I get the same answer as when I add 6 to the number and then treble the result.

5 If I multiply the number by 7, subtract 5 and then multiply the result 2, the answer I get is the same as when I multiply the number by 11 and then add 20.

6

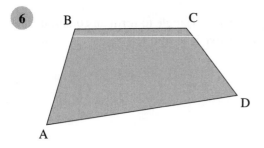

B   C

A

D

The angles of a quadrilateral are A, B, C and D. Angle B is twice as big as angle A. Angle C is 30° bigger than angle A and angle D is 10° smaller than angle A. Find the size of angle A.

7 In the triangle, PR is three times as long as PQ. QR is 30 cm longer than PQ. Find the length PQ if the perimeter of the triangle is 105 cm.

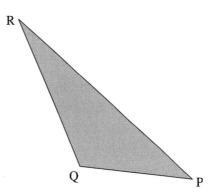

8 Angle A in this isosceles triangle is 60° more than angle B. Find the actual values of the three angles.

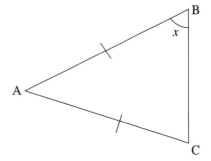

9 Sophie is 15 years younger than Ed. Kelly is treble Sophie's age. The sum of Sophie's and Ed's ages is equal to Kelly's age. How old is Sophie?

10

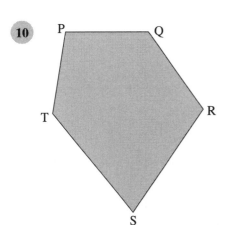

The angles in a pentagon add up to 540°.

Angle T is 10° more than angle S which is 10° more than angle R which is 10° more than angle Q which is 10° more than angle P.

Find the value of angle P.

2.5 Estimating

Do not use a calculator. Decide, by estimating, which of the three answers is closest to the exact value. Write the letter A, B or C for each part.

	Calculation	A	B	C
1	39.2×58.6	240	1500	2400
2	10.16×19.73	200	50	400
3	71.4×20.18	1400	70	3000
4	$51.62 \div 4.89$	50	1	10
5	$109.7 \div 2.03$	50	20	150
6	$596.1 \div 31.37$	5	20	200
7	0.98×29.42	1.5	180	30
8	81.73×20.76	800	1600	80
9	3.01×5.14	25	15	1.5
10	40.9×69.3	700	5600	2800
11	$319.2 \div 78.64$	2	40	4
12	$1512 \div 48.93$	30	10	300
13	$20.07 \times 0.98 \times 10.36$	100	400	200
14	8.8^2	80	65	160
15	$14.26 \div 27.85$	2	0.5	0.1
16	$0.99 \times 1.04 \times 0.97$	3	1	0.5
17	$\sqrt{15.8} \times 9.83$	40	20	100
18	49% of 3016	150	1500	15000
19	$18.174 + 11.68$	25	30	40
20	0.94% of £312	£310	£31	£3
21	$\sqrt{99} \div \sqrt{3.899}$	5	2.5	30
22	$89.138 - 20.046$	70	110	30
23	$\dfrac{3.01 + 46.8}{10.17}$	7	100	5
24	$\dfrac{6.99^2 + 19.65}{0.52}$	90	140	35

Do not use a calculator for these questions.

1 Seventy-nine people each pay £14.95 for a local theatre ticket. Roughly how much do they pay in total?

2 Tyrone works for half a year at a holiday resort. He earns £390 each week. Roughly how much does he earn in total?

3 A group of 22 people win £351000 on the Lottery. Give a rough estimate for how much money each person receives.

4 Cherie buys 2 cartons of soup, one chicken, 6 tins of beans and 2 boxes of dog food.

Estimate how much change she will get from £30.

tin of beans	48p
loaf of bread	£1.09
carton of soup	£1.89
one chicken	£7.15
box of dog food	£4.95

5 A wall is 1.79 metres high. There are 31 rows of bricks, Estimate the height of each brick.

6 There are nine calculations and nine answers below. Write down each calculation and choose the correct answer from the list given.

(a) 2.1×19.8

(b) 82.1×3.9

(c) $47.38 \div 4$

(d) 4.9×4.8

(e) $31.08 \div 5$

(f) $2.12 + 7.83$

(g) $68.92 \div 2$

(h) 11% of 560

(i) 52.1×0.98

Answers	23.52	61.6	11.845
	34.46	41.58	51.058
	9.95	6.216	320.19

7 A plant grows 0.09 cm each day. Roughly how much does it grow during February, March and April?

8 Give an estimate for each of the following calculations.

(a) $\dfrac{3.02 \times 30.1}{9.97}$

(b) 73% of 35.9 kg

(c) $\dfrac{15.16 + 4.88}{4.09}$

(d) $\dfrac{41.07 - 12.1}{5.13}$

(e) $\dfrac{9.86 \times 29.43}{0.489}$

(f) $\dfrac{19.6 \times 30.23}{41.12 + 9.07}$

2.6 Fully functional 1

Petra is planning to throw a big party. She wants to provide good food with a waiter service.

She needs 2 chefs, 3 waiters and one person to wash and clear up.

She knows 7 people who can do some of these jobs. They each charge different hourly rates,

depending on which job they are doing. The table below provides all this information.

Name	Job	hourly rate
Terry	Junior chef	£7
	Waiter 2	£6.80
Maggie	Waiter 1	£6.50
Simon	Waiter 1	£6.80
	Waiter 2	£6.50
Laura	Main chef	£9.15
	Junior chef	£7
	Washer	£8.25
Darryl	Main chef	£9.20
Buffy	Main waiter	£9
Reece	Junior chef	£7.50
	Main waiter	£9.20

Petra needs to choose 6 people only to do the 6 jobs (Main waiter, waiter 1, waiter 2, washer, Main chef and Junior chef). They will each work for 8 hours and Petra needs to spend the least amount of money possible. Who should Petra choose for each job and how much will she pay in total for the 8 hours?

Show your working out clearly.

UNIT 3

3.1 Drawing graphs and $y = mx + c$

1 (a) Copy and complete the table for $y = 2x + 2$

x	0	1	2	3	4	5
$2x$	0	2	4			
$+2$	2	2				
y	2	4				

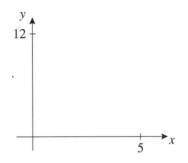

(b) Draw the graph using the axes shown.

2 (a) Make a table similar to the one above for the graph of $y = 3x + 2$. Take x from 0 to 5.

(b) Draw the graph of $y = 3x + 2$.

3 (a) Copy and complete the table for $y = 2x - 4$.

x	-2	-1	0	1	2	3
$2x$	-4	-2				
-4	-4	-4			-4	
y	-8	-6				

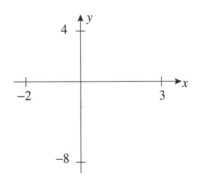

(b) Draw the graph using the axes shown.

4 Draw $y = 3x - 1$ for x-values from -3 to 3.

5 (a) Draw an x-axis from 0 to 5 and a y-axis from 0 to 16.

(b) On the same graph, draw the lines $y = 2x + 6$ and $y = 12 - x$

(c) Write down the coordinates of the point where the two lines intersect each other.

36

Remember: $(-2)^2 = -2 \times -2 = 4$ *not* -4
$(-3)^2 - (-3) = 9 + 3 = 12$

1 (a) Copy and complete the table for $y = x^2 + 1$

x	−3	−2	−1	0	1	2	3
x^2	9	4					
+1	1	1	1				
y	10						

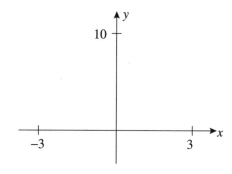

(b) Draw the graph using the axes shown.

2 (a) Make a table like the one above for the curve $y = x^2 - 2$, for x values from −3 to 3.

(b) Draw the curve and write down the coordinates of the two points where the curve cuts the x-axis.

3 (a) Copy and complete the table for $y = x^2 + 3x$

x	−5	−4	−3	−2	−1	0	1	2
x^2	25							4
$3x$	−15	−12						6
y	10							10

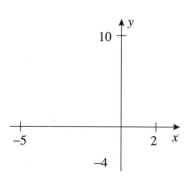

(b) Draw the graph using the axes shown.

4 Draw the graph of $y = x^2 + 4x - 3$ for x-values from −5 to 1.

Remember: gradient of a line = $\dfrac{\text{difference between } y \text{ coordinates}}{\text{difference between } x \text{ coordinates}}$

1 Find the gradient of:

(a) line AB

(b) line CD

(c) line EF

(d) line GH

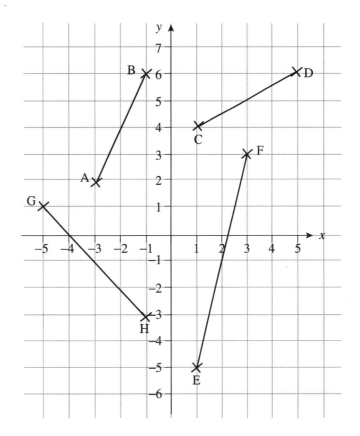

2 Find the gradient of the line joining

(a) (4, 2) and (6, 10)

(b) (2, 1) and (5, 22)

(c) (1, 3) and (3, 5)

(d) (2, 4) and (6, 16)

(e) (2, 5) and (4, 6)

(f) (1, −4) and (−2, 2)

(g) (−3, −5) and (1, −1)

(h) (4, −3) and (−1, 27)

3 Answer true or false:

'The line joining (−3, 2) and (2, 17) is parallel to the line joining (4, −6) and (6, 0).'

4 Find the gradient of the line joining:

(a) P and Q

(b) Q and R

(c) P and R

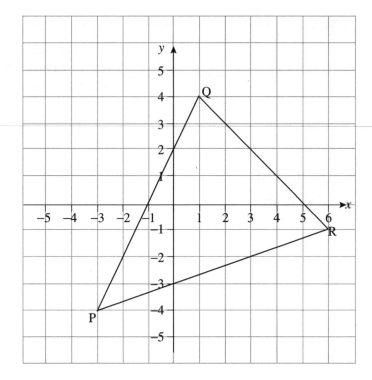

HWK 2E ———————————————————————— **Main Book Page 98**

> Remember: The y-intercept of a line is where the line
> crosses the y-axis.

1 On the same axes, draw the graphs of $y = 2x + 1$, $y = 2x + 5$ and $y = 2x - 3$.

(a) Find the gradient of each line.

(b) Write down the y-intercept of each line.

(c) Write down what you notice about each line and its equation.

2 Repeat question **1** for the graphs of $y = -3x$, $y = -3x + 2$ and $y = -3x + 4$.

3 Write down the gradient of $y = 4x + 5$.

4 Write down the gradient of $y = 6x - 2$.

5 Where do you expect the line $y = 5x - 3$ to cut the y-axis?

6 Write down the equation of any line parallel to $y = 5x + 2$.

Write down the gradient and *y*-intercept of each of the following lines:

1 $y = 4x - 1$ **2** $y = 2x + 9$ **3** $y = -4x + 3$

4 $y = \frac{1}{3}x + 6$ **5** $y = \frac{1}{4}x - 3$ **6** $y = -x - 2$

7 $y = 3 - 2x$ **8** $y = 6 + 4x$ **9** $y = 4 - \frac{1}{3}x$

In questions **10** to **15** match each sketch with the correct equation from the list below.

10 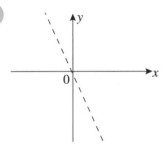 **11** 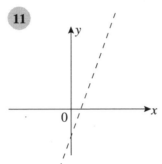 **12**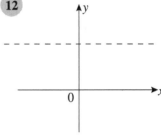

13 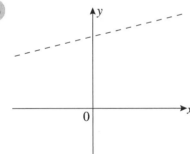 **14** 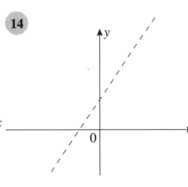 **15**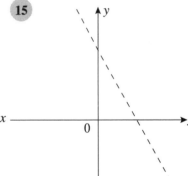

(a) $y = 3x + 1$ (b) $y = -2x$ (c) $y = \frac{1}{2}x + 5$

(d) $y = 4 - 2x$ (e) $y = 3$ (f) $y = 4x - 2$

16 Write down the equation of any line parallel to $y = x - 7$.

17 Write down the equation of any line parallel to $y = 2 - 6x$.

18 Write down which of the two lines below meet at the same point on the *y*-axis.

$\boxed{y = 4x + 3}$ $\boxed{y = 3x + 4}$ $\boxed{y = 3 - 2x}$

19 Which of the lines below are parallel to $y = 5x - 1$?

$\boxed{y = 2 + 5x}$ $\boxed{y = -5x + 3}$ $\boxed{y = 5x - 8}$ $\boxed{y = -5x - 1}$

20 A line crosses the *y*-axis at (0, –2) and has a gradient equal to 4. Write down the equation of this line.

3.2 Area

1 Work out the area of each shape and write down the shapes in order of size, starting with the smallest.

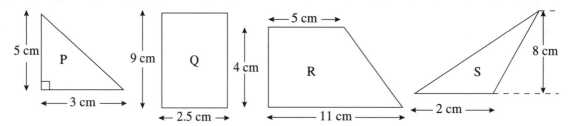

2 The area of this triangle is 72 cm². Write down the value of length *x*.

3 Find the total shaded area.

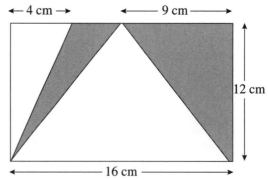

4 Find the area of the shape.

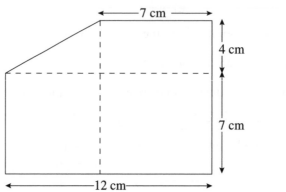

5

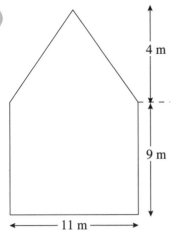

Shula paints one wall on the outside of her house as shown.

Each minute she paints 0.4 m². How long does it take her to paint the whole wall? (Give your answer in hours and minutes)

HWK 2M	**Main Book Page 103**

Remember:

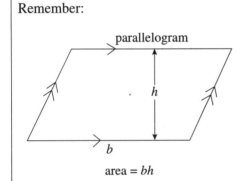

parallelogram

area = bh

trapezium

area = $\frac{1}{2}(a + b) \times h$

1 Work out the area of each shape and write down the shapes in order of size, starting with the smallest.

(a)

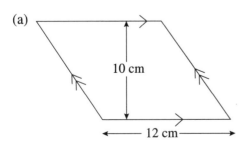

10 cm

12 cm

(b)

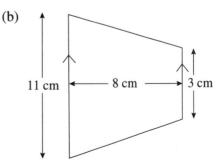

11 cm   8 cm   3 cm

42

(c)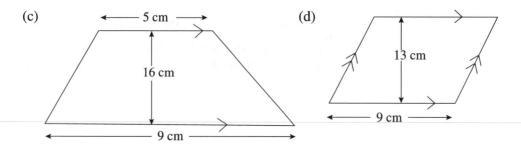

(d)

2 A trapezium has parallel sides of length 15 cm and 11 cm. Find the distance between the parallel sides if the area of the trapezium is 39 cm².

3 Find the total area of the shape below:

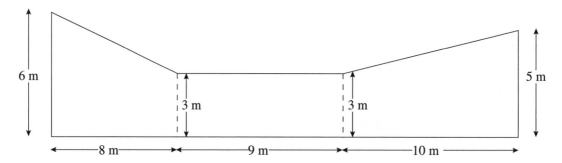

4 A parallelogram has an area of 75 m². Find the base length if its height is 150 m?

5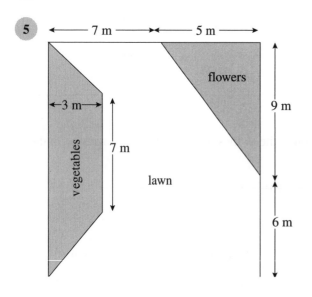

Calculate the area of the lawn in Mark's garden.

6 Use the information below to calculate the total area of shape ABCDEFGH.

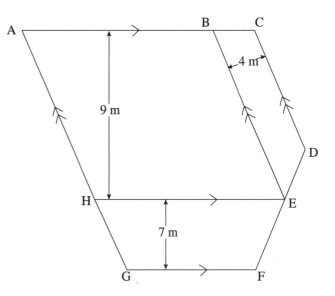

AB = 12 m   BE = 10 m

BC = 5 m   HE = 12 m

CD = 7 m   AH = 10 m

DE = 5 m   HG = 8 m

EF = 8 m   GF = 10 m

HWK 2E   **Main Book Page 104**

1

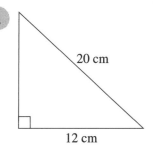

The perimeter of this triangle is 48 cm. What is the area of the triangle?

2 A bathroom wall measures 3 m by 2.5 m. Martin wants to tile the whole wall. Each tile measures 10 cm by 10 cm. The tiles come in boxes of 50.

(a) How many boxes must Martin buy?

(b) Unfortunately Martin breaks 10% of the tiles during the work. How many more boxes must Martin buy to finish the job?

3 Calculate the shaded area shown opposite.

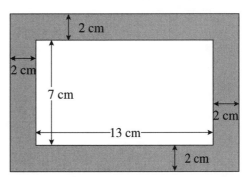

4 A rectangular park has an area of 108 hectares. Calculate the width of the park if its length is 1.2 km. (1 hectare = 10000 m²)

5

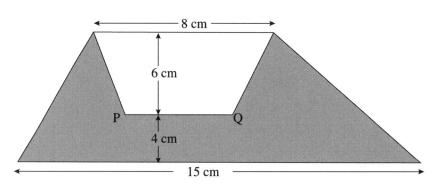

The area of this triangle is 60 cm².
Calculate the length AB.

6 Calculate the shaded area if PQ = 5 cm.

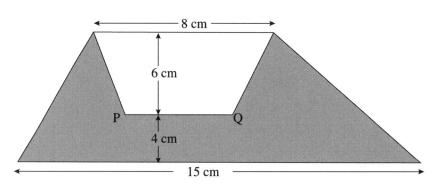

7 A rectangular swimming pool 20 m by 9 m is surrounded by a path 1.5 m wide. What is the area of the path?

8

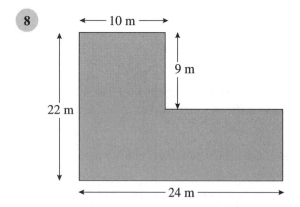

This floor is carpeted with Tamworth Twist carpet which costs £18.79 per square metre. Find the total cost if an extra 5% of carpet is allowed for to be safe? (Give your answer to the nearest penny)

3.3 Transformations

> Remember: the translation vector $\begin{pmatrix} -4 \\ 2 \end{pmatrix}$ means the shape moves 4 units to the left and 2 units up

1

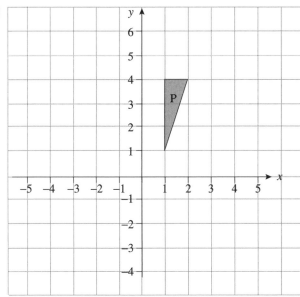

Copy this diagram.

(a) Translate shape P with the vector $\begin{pmatrix} -4 \\ -3 \end{pmatrix}$. Label the new shape Q.

(b) Translate shape P with the vector $\begin{pmatrix} 3 \\ -4 \end{pmatrix}$. Label the new shape R.

(c) Translate shape P with the vector $\begin{pmatrix} 2 \\ 2 \end{pmatrix}$. Label the new shape S.

(d) Write down the vector which will translate:

   (i)   shape Q onto shape R

   (ii)   shape S onto shape Q

   (iii) shape R onto shape S

2 Look at the diagram opposite.
Write down the vector for each of
the following translations:

(a) A → E   (b) B → F

(c) F → E   (d) H → D

(e) B → G   (f) D → C

(g) C → G   (h) D → A

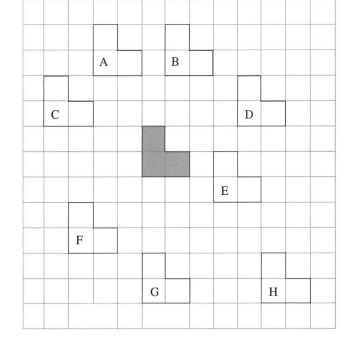

1 Write down the equation of the mirror line for each reflection.

(a) ΔT → ΔW

(b) ΔR → ΔP

(c) ΔU → ΔR

(d) ΔQ → ΔS

(e) ΔV → ΔT

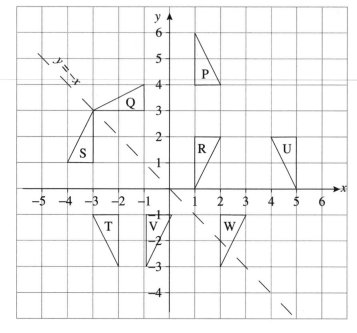

2 Copy the axes from question **1** and triangle Q only. Rotate triangle Q 90° clockwise about the origin (0, 0). (You may use tracing paper if you have any)

3

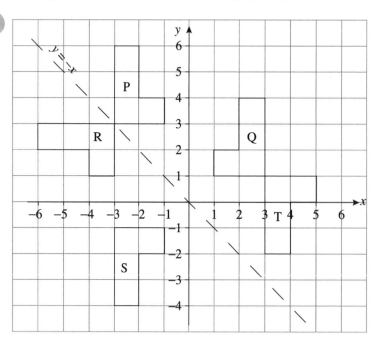

Describe fully each of the following transformations.

(a) T → S

(b) Q → T

(c) P → R

(d) S → P

4 (a) Draw axes with x and y from –6 to +6.

(b) Draw a rectangle with vertices at (–1, 2), (–4, 2), (–4, 3) and (–1, 3). Label this as shape A.

(c) Rotate shape A 90° clockwise about (0, 1). Label the new shape B.

(d) Reflect shape B in the line $y = x$. Label the new shape C.

(e) Translate shape C with vector $\begin{pmatrix} -1 \\ -4 \end{pmatrix}$. Label the new shape D.

(f) Reflect shape D in the line $x = -1$. Label the new shape E.

(g) Describe fully the transformation which maps shape E onto shape A.

HWK 2M ──────────────────────────────── **Main Book Page 113**

1 Copy each shape with its centre of enlargement. Enlarge the shape by the scale factor given.

(a)

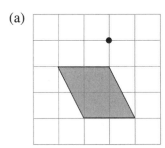

scale factor 2

(b)

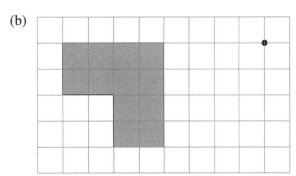

scale factor $\frac{1}{2}$

(c)

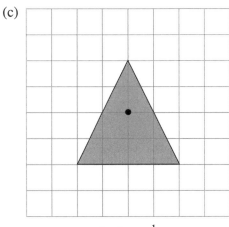

scale factor $\frac{1}{2}$

(d)

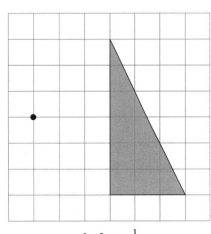

scale factor $\frac{1}{3}$

48

2 Describe fully each of the following enlargements.

(a) shape P → shape Q

(b) shape R → shape S

(c) shape Q → shape P

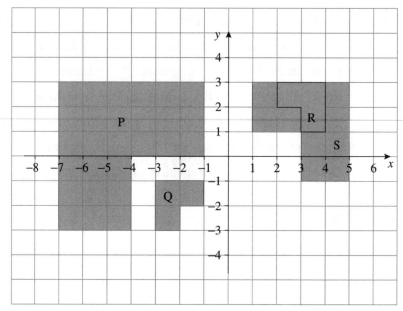

3 (a) Draw an *x*-axis from –5 to 7.
Draw a *y*-axis from –2 to 5.

(b) Draw a triangle with vertices at (0, 4), (6, 4) and (6, 0).

(c) Enlarge this triangle by scale factor $\frac{1}{2}$ about (–4, 4).

HWK 2E ──────────────────────── **Main Book Page 114**

1 (a) Draw an *x*-axis from –8 to 5.
Draw a *y*-axis from –5 to 5.

(b) Draw a triangle with vertices at (3, 1), (3, 2) and (1, 2). Label this as triangle P.

(c) Enlarge triangle P by scale factor 2 about (3, 0). Label the new triangle Q.

(d) Reflect triangle Q in the line *x* = –2. Label the new triangle R.

(e) Translate triangle R with vector $\begin{pmatrix} 0 \\ -3 \end{pmatrix}$. Label the new triangle S.

(f) Rotate triangle S 90° anticlockwise about (–2, 1). Label the new triangle T.

(g) Rotate triangle T 90° clockwise about (0, –4). Label the new triangle U.

(h) Describe fully the transformation which maps triangle U onto triangle R.

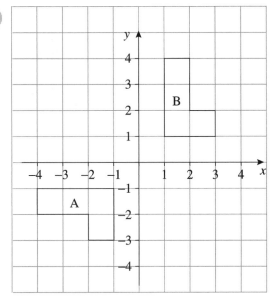

(a) Shape A is transformed into shape B by a reflection followed by a rotation about the origin. Describe these two transformations as fully as possible.

(b) Shape A can be mapped onto shape B by a *single* transformation. Describe this transformation as fully as possible.

3 (a) Shape A is transformed into shape B by a translation followed by a rotation about the origin. Describe these two transformations as fully as possible.

(b) Would the image be the same if the rotation was completed before the translation?

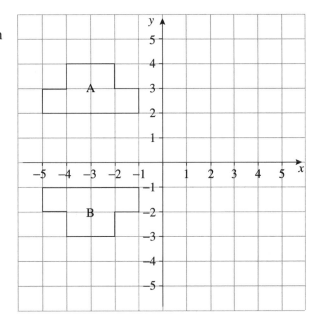

3.4 Charts and graphs

1 Two groups of people take 20 penalties in a football competition. The charts below show how many penalties were scored.

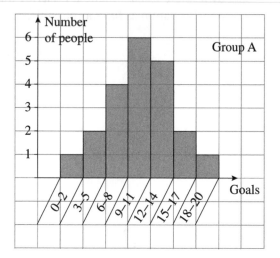
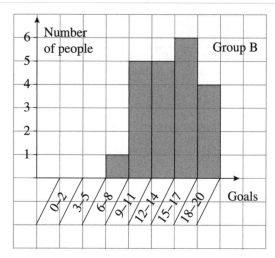

(a) How many people in group A scored less then 12 goals?

(b) One group was a mixture of people but the other group was made up from regular professional footballers. State which group had the professional footballers. Give your evidence for making this choice.

2 This frequency diagram shows the weights of a group of children.

(a) How many children are there in total?

(b) What fraction of the children weigh between 50 kg and 55 kg?

(c) Draw your own frequency diagram that shows a group of children who *generally* weigh more than the children shown in the frequency diagram opposite.

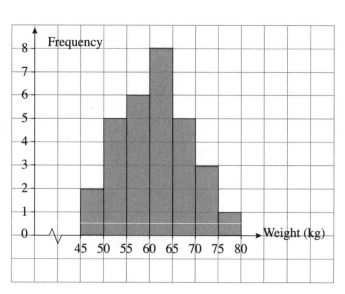

3 Thirty children take a maths exam. Their percentage results are shown below.

61	34	82	50	48	68
87	53	64	76	70	58
66	46	70	37	84	69
71	75	98	60	57	78
89	60	50	61	65	74

(a) Put the marks into groups.

class interval	frequency
$30 \leq m < 40$	
$40 \leq m < 50$	
$50 \leq m < 60$	

(The group '$30 \leq m < 40$' means marks greater than or equal to 30 and less than 40)

(b) Draw a frequency diagram.

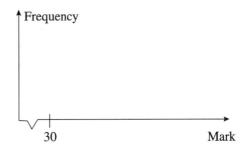

(c) The pass mark for the test was 50. What fraction of the children failed the test?

4 Three classes raise money for charity.
Jack says 'More children raised money for charity in class 9B than in class 9A'.
Is he correct or not? *Explain* your answer *fully*.

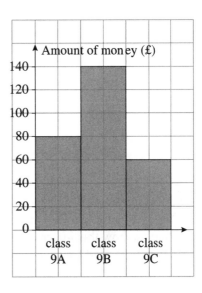

1

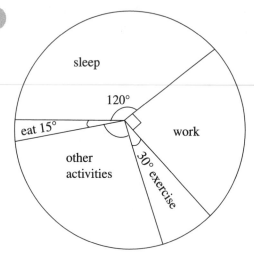

This pie chart shows how Carly spends an average Friday doing activity from midnight to midnight.

How many hours does she spend:

(a) working?

(b) doing exercise?

(c) sleeping?

(d) doing other activities?

2 240 people were asked to taste four different flavoured ice creams. They were then asked which was their favourite flavour. The results are shown in the pie chart.

(a) How many people chose vanilla?

(b) How many people chose strawberry?

(c) How many more people chose chocolate than mint?

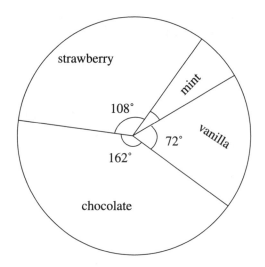

3 The table opposite shows the percentage of notes made for each party in a General Election. Draw a pie chart to show this information (indicate clearly the angle used for each party).

Party	Percentage
Labour	35
Conservative	30
Liberal Democrats	20
Green Party	5
Others	10

4 A small company has 45 people working for it.

Job	Number of People
office	7
workshop	18
transport	12
sales	8

Draw a pie chart to show the proportion of people working in each job as shown opposite.

5 120 people were asked what building for entertainment they would like to see built in Hexford. The results are shown opposite.

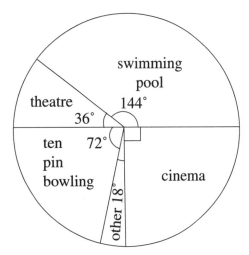

200 people were asked what building for entertainment they would like to see built in Atherton. The results are shown opposite.

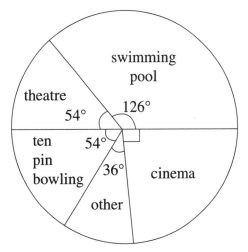

(a) 'More people in Hexford than in Atherton want a swimming pool'. True or false? Give a clear reason for your answer.

(b) 'The same number of people in Hexford and Atherton want a cinema'. True or false? Give a clear reason for your answer.

54

3.5 Drawing and visualising 3D shapes

1 Draw an accurate net for the triangular prism shown opposite.

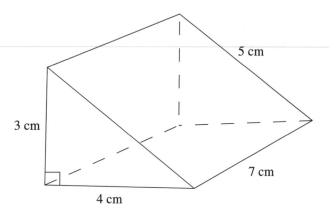

3 cm

5 cm

7 cm

4 cm

2 How many planes of symmetry does the triangular prism in question **1** have?

3 Draw a cube made from twenty-seven 1 cm cubes.

4 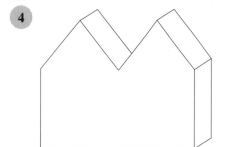   How many planes of symmetry does this solid have?

5 Draw a solid which has three planes of symmetry only.

6

(a) Draw a diagram of side-view A.

(b) Draw a diagram of side-view B.

Side-view B

Side-view A

7 Draw a plan view and a side view of a cone.

3.6 Volume

Remember: volume of a prism = (area of cross section) × length

1 Find the volume of each prism.

(a)

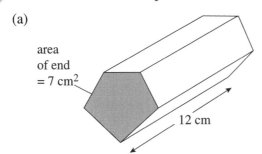

area of end = 7 cm²

12 cm

(b)

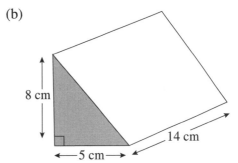

8 cm

5 cm

14 cm

(c)

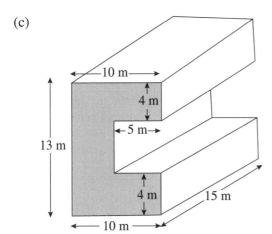

10 m

4 m

5 m

13 m

4 m

15 m

10 m

(d)

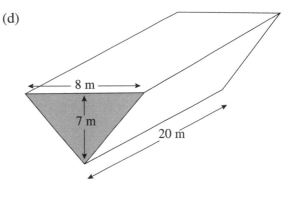

8 m

7 m

20 m

2

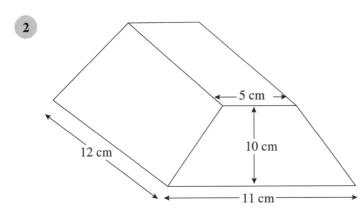

5 cm

10 cm

12 cm

11 cm

Beth has 15 prisms identical to the one shown opposite. Calculate the total volume of all 15 prisms.

3

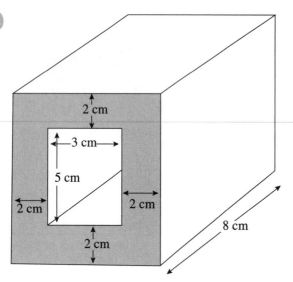

2 cm

3 cm

5 cm

2 cm   2 cm

2 cm

8 cm

The middle of a piece of wood is removed as shown.

Calculate the volume of the remaining wood.

HWK 1E   **Main Book Page 128**

Remember: 1 m³ = 1000 litres

1

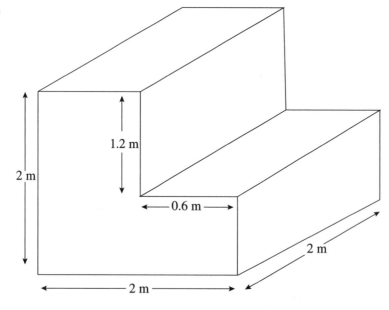

1.2 m

2 m

0.6 m

2 m

2 m

Find the capacity, in litres, of this prism.

2 Find the capacity, in litres, of a rectangular container with internal dimensions 80 cm by 40 cm by 1.5 m.

3

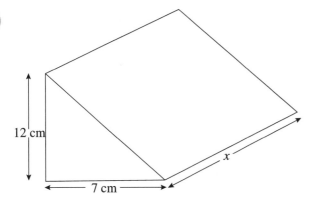

12 cm

7 cm

x

The volume of this triangular prism is 672 cm³.

Calculate the length *x*.

4 Calculate the *surface area* of each prism below.

(a)

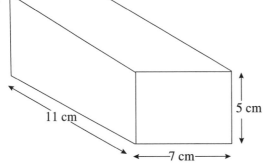

11 cm

7 cm

5 cm

(b)

15 cm

20 cm

12 cm

9 cm

5 The capacity of this container is 23400 litres.

Calculate the length *x*.

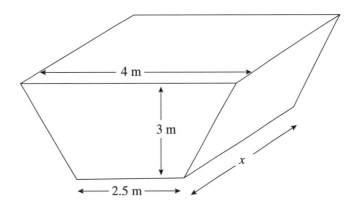

4 m

3 m

2.5 m

x

Give answers correct to 1 decimal place where necessary.

1 Find the volume of each cylinder.

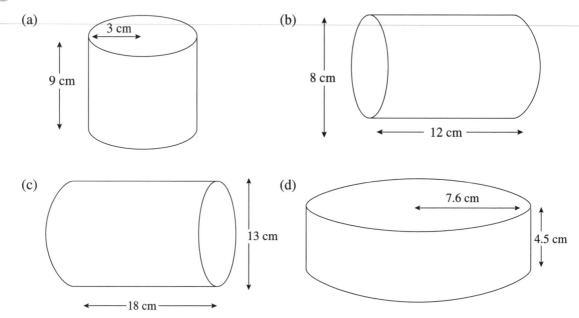

(a) 3 cm 9 cm

(b) 8 cm 12 cm

(c) 13 cm 18 cm

(d) 7.6 cm 4.5 cm

2 A cylindrical cake has diameter 24 cm and is 8 cm thick. What is the volume of the cake?

3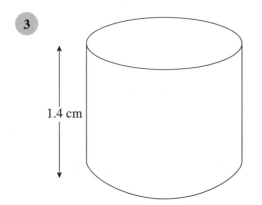

This container has diameter 0.92 m.
Calculate the capacity of the container in litres.

1.4 cm

4 A stick of rock is a cylindrical shape. It has a radius of 1.9 cm. What is the length of the stick of rock if its volume is 295 cm³?

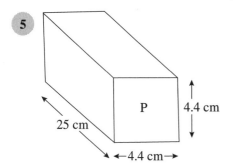

5

P   4.4 cm

25 cm

←4.4 cm→

Which prism has the larger
volume and by how much?

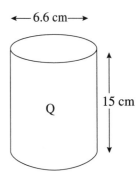

←6.6 cm→

Q   15 cm

| HWK 2E | Main Book Page 132 |

Give answers correct to 1 decimal place where necessary.

1 Cylinders are cut along the axis of symmetry. Find the volume of each object.

(a)

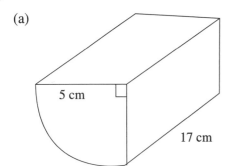

5 cm

17 cm

(b)

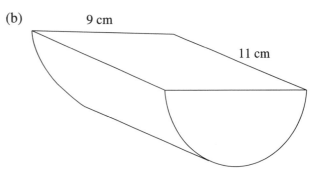

9 cm

11 cm

2 A cylindrical glass has diameter 9 cm and height 10 cm. A carton of juice in the shape of a
cuboid measures 25 cm × 16 cm × 9 cm.
How many times can the glass be completely filled with juice?

3

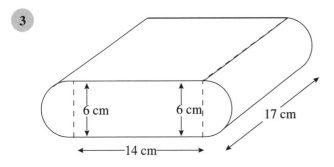

6 cm   6 cm   17 cm

←14 cm→

This diagram shows a case for binoculars.
The front end is made from a rectangle
and two semicircles as shown.
Calculate the volume of this case.

4 This container is filled with water at a rate of 200 ml per second. How long does it take to fill the tank completely? (Give your answer to the nearest minute)

Remember: 1 m³ = 1000 litres and
            1 litre = 1000 ml

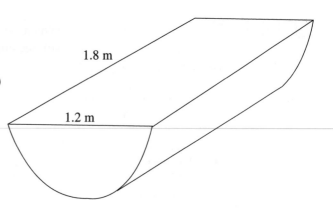

1.8 m

1.2 m

5

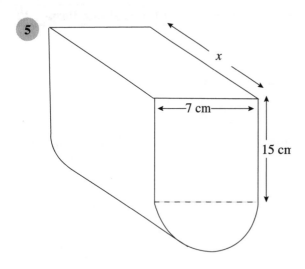

x

7 cm

15 cm

The volume of this prism is 2236 cm³. Calculate the length x.

UNIT 4

4.1 Percentages

> Remember: £5.27613 = £5.28 (to the nearest penny)
>
> '34 out of 80 as a percentage' $= \dfrac{34}{80} \times 100 = 42.5\%$

You may use a calculator.

1 Work out

(a) 14% of £275   (b) 8% of £19.20   (c) 3.5% of £290

2 Change these fractions to percentages

(a) $\dfrac{3}{5}$ (b) $\dfrac{17}{20}$ (c) $\dfrac{231}{600}$ (d) $\dfrac{317}{500}$

3 350 children from England, Ireland, Scotland and Wales attend a special schools' conference. 46% of the children come from England and 8% of them come from Ireland. Four times as many children come from Scotland as from Ireland. How many children come from Wales?

4 A driving instructor recorded how many people passed their driving test and whether it was their first, second or third attempt at the test.

	Pass	Fail
1st Attempt	48	57
2nd Attempt	36	21
3rd Attempt	13	8

(a) What percentage of the people passed their driving test at the first attempt?
Give your answer to one decimal place.

(b) What percentage of the people failed their driving test at the second attempt?
Give your answer to one decimal place.

5 Jack and Kelly sold items at a car boot sale. It was agreed that Jack should keep 45% of any money taken. Exactly how much money does he keep if they take £86.84 in total?

6 A group of 4 friends go out for a pizza. They agree to give the waiter a tip which is 15% of the cost of the meal.
How much will each person give towards the tip if the cost of the meal is £67.24?

7

	Fraction	Decimal	Percentage
(a)	$\dfrac{9}{25}$		
(b)			4%
(c)	$\dfrac{1}{5}$		
(d)		0.65	

Copy and complete the table.

8 The table below shows how many boys and girls there are in five year 9 classes in Henton High School. What percentage of all the children in year 9 are girls? Give your answer to one decimal place.

class	9A	9B	9C	9D	9E
boys	17	15	17	13	14
girls	14	15	18	18	16

HWK 1E ———————————————————— **Main Book Page 149**

You may use a calculator.

1 (a) Reduce £620 by 5%.

(b) Decrease 70 kg by 45%.

(c) Increase 8400 g by 80%.

2 Rachel buys an electric keyboard for £184. It loses 65% of its value over the next three years. How much is the keyboard worth after three years?

3 Mr Webb breeds rabbits. In March he has 16 rabbits. By the end of August the number of rabbits has increased by 87.5% . He then sells 9 rabbits. How many rabbits does the man now have?

4 Alice, Tyrone, Ken and Mel each invest money in some banks. The table opposite shows how much money each person invests and what percentage increase they get over the next 3 years.

Write out the names of the people in the order of how much money they have in the bank after 3 years, starting with the largest.

Name	Amount Invested	% increase
Alice	£1800	11
Tyrone	£1450	39
Ken	£2000	8.5
Mel	£1925	13

5 Gemma's flat was worth £178 000 at the start of 2008. It gained 4% in value during 2008.

(a) How much was Gemma's flat worth at the end of 2008?

(b) During 2009 the flat lost 4% of its value at the end of 2008. How much was Gemma's flat worth at the end of 2009?

6 Harris and his sister both have £60 to spend. Harris spends 70% of his money and his sister spends £45. Who has the most money left and by how much?

> Remember: % increase = $\left(\dfrac{\text{actual increase}}{\text{original value}}\right) \times 100$

Give answers correct to 1 decimal place, where necessary.

1. The price of a car drops from £7200 to £4200. What is the percentage decrease?

2. On average, Magnus gets 6 hours sleep each night. He decides to change his sleep pattern and manages to increase his sleep to 7 hours each night. What is the percentage increase in his hours of sleep each night?

3.

	Original price	Final price
(a)	£350	£280
(b)	£280	£392
(c)	£23	£30
(d)	£118.30	£75.50

Calculate the percentage increase or decrease in each case.

4. Jen used to weigh 63 kg but now weighs 59 kg. What is the percentage decrease in her weight?

5. Jerome buys a table for £190 and sells it for £250. Shania buys a sofa for £350 and sells it for £470. Who makes the larger percentage profit and by what percentage greater is it?

6. Calculate the percentage reduction in price for each item shown opposite in a sale.

	item	original price	sale price
(a)	chair	£267	£189
(b)	cupboard	£204	£155
(c)	coffee table	£186	£99.50
(d)	wardrobe	£312	£225

Give answers correct to 1 decimal place, where necessary.

1. Tim buys 350 games at £6 each. He manages to sell 260 of the games at £10 each. He eventually sells off the other 90 games at £3 each. What was Tim's overall perentage profit?

2. Elouise buys a car for £8000. After 4 years the car is worth 60% less than this. Her cousin pays £500 more than this value for the car. Work out the percentage loss for Elouise.

3 Find the percentage profit or loss for each item below.

camera
cost price £60
selling price £81

shirt
cost price £32
selling price £25

computer
cost price £380
selling price £550

4 Rory buys 80 cauliflowers at 55p each and sells them all for a total of £60. He also buys 75 cabbages at 45p each and sells 60 of them at 95p each. He has to throw away the remaining cabbages. Calculate Rory's overall percentage profit.

5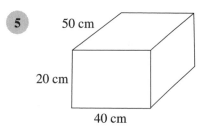

50 cm

20 cm

40 cm

(a) Work out the total surface area of this cuboid.

(b) Each measurement is increased by 10%. Calculate the new total surface area of the cuboid.

(c) What is the percentage increase in the surface area of the cuboid?

6 This chart shows the number of patients seen by a doctor in each of 4 weeks.

	Week 1	Week 2	Week 3	Week 4	Total
under 16	46	58	47	68	219
16 to 65	57	67	35	89	248
over 65	71	68	69	59	267
Total	174	193	151	216	734

(a) What was the percentage increase in the number of patients seen in week 4 compared to week 3?

(b) What was the percentage decrease in the number of under 16's seen in week 3 compared to week 2?

(c) What was the percentage increase in the number of 16 to 65 year old patients seen in week 4 compared to week 1?

You may use a calculator.

1 A train ticket costs £89.38 after a 9% increase in prices. What was the price of the ticket before the increase?

2 Zoe earns £33800 after a 4% pay increase. How much did she earn before the increase?

3 The bird population in a certain area is estimated to be 10209. This suggests that the population has fallen by 17%. What was the size of the population before this decrease?

4 An investor loses 29% of his money on the Stock Market. He now has £227200 left. How much money did he have before the loss?

5 Find the old price for each of the following items:

	Item	Old price	New price	% change
(a)	Shirt	?	£33.60	20% increase
(b)	Radio	?	£59.40	8% increase
(c)	Chair	?	£136	15% decrease
(d)	Table	?	£240.50	26% decrease
(e)	Skirt	?	£47.04	12% increase
(f)	Clock	?	£33.15	35% decrease

You may use a calculator.

1 The number of road accidents in an area is 578 during one year. This is a 15% decrease compared to the previous year. How many road accidents were there during the previous year?

2 The number of people staying at hotels in the seaside resort of Barton in 2010 is 144336. This is a 7% decrease on the number in 2009 which was a 3% decrease on the number in 2008. How many people stayed at the hotels in 2008?

3 VAT (Value Added Tax) of 17.5% is added to the cost of a TV. The total cost is £752. How much does the TV cost before the VAT is added?

4 What is the cost of this camera without the VAT being included? (VAT is 17.5%)

Camera

£242.05

(including VAT)

5 Two boxers are 'bulking' up for a fight. During the two weeks leading up to the fight,

Menzie puts on an extra 6% weight and Larry increases his weight by 8%. Menzie weighs 108.12 kg and Larry weighs 107.46 kg at the start of the fight.

Who weighed the most two weeks before the fight and by how much?

6

| Freeandeasy |
| Cereal |
| 13% fibre |

A box of cereal contains 35.1 g of fibre. What is the total weight of the box of cereal?

7 Kelly writes a book. She has written 169 pages which is 65% of the pages that she eventually writes. How many pages are in the book when it is completed?

8 A gas bill is £39.69 which includes VAT at 5%. A unit of gas costs 9p before the VAT is added. How many units of gas were used to produce this bill?

4.2 Equations Review

| HWK 1M | Main Book Page 156 |

Solve the equations

1 $5x + 3 = 38$

2 $7x - 10 = 18$

3 $4x - 12 = 28$

4 $15 = 7x - 6$

5 $4x + 13 = 2x + 29$

6 $3x + 2 = 5x - 28$

7 $6x - 9 = 2x + 35$

8 $2x + 39 = 4x + 3$

9 $15 + 6x = 16x - 5$

10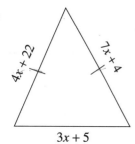

(a) Write down an equation involving x for this isosceles triangle.

(b) Find x.

(c) Find the actual perimeter of the triangle. All lengths are in cm.

Now solve these equations

11 $5(2x + 3) = 35$

12 $2(3x + 1) = 50$

13 $3(4x - 8) = 120$

14 $8(3x - 7) = 64$

15 $180 = 6(3x + 9)$

16 $27 = 9(10x - 7)$

| HWK 1E | Main Book Page 156 |

Solve the equations

1 $6x - 4 = 1$

2 $7 = 5x + 3$

3 $5 + 2x = 8$

4 $7x + 9 = 4x + 11$

5 $8x - 10 = 4x + 1$

6 $9 + 3x = 14 - 3x$

7 $13 = 6 + 2x$

8 $8x + 7 = 3x + 7$

9 $12 - 4x = 9 + 7x$

10 The distance from Garside to Corton is equal to the distance from Corton to Ambleton. Find the value of x then write down the total distance from Garside to Ambleton. Assume all distances are in miles.

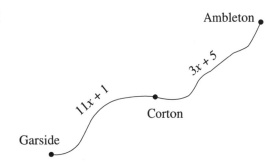

Ambleton

$3x + 5$

Corton

$11x + 1$

Garside

Now solve these equations:

11 $4(3x + 5) = 25$

12 $2(5 + 2x) = 6$

13 $5(3x + 1) = 7(x + 3)$

14 $3(2x - 3) = 5(x + 4)$

15 $8 = 2(2x - 5)$

16 $5(2x + 5) = 2(4x + 11)$

HWK 2M   **Main Book Page 158**

1 The area of this rectangle is 60 cm².

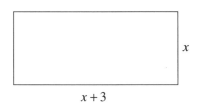

x

$x + 3$

trial	calculation $x(x + 3)$	too large or too small?
$x = 7$	$7 \times 10 = \ldots$	too large
$x = 6$	$6 \times 9 = \ldots$	too small
$x = 6.5$	$6.5 \times 9.5 = \ldots$	too ...
$x = 6.2$	$6.2 \times 9.2 = \ldots$	too ...
$x = 6.4$	$6.4 \times 9.4 = \ldots$	too ...
$x = 6.3$	$6.3 \times 9.3 = \ldots$	too ...
So $x = \ldots$ cm to 1 decimal place		

Copy and complete this table to find x to one decimal place.

2 Use trial and improvement for each rectangle below to find the value of x to 1 decimal place.

(a)

area = 42 cm²

x

$x + 4$

(b)

area = 31 cm²

x

$x + 6$

3 A rectangular room has an area of 58 m². The length of the room is 4.5 m greater than the width of the room. Find the width of the room correct to one decimal place.

1 Use trial and improvement to solve the equations, correct to 1 decimal place.

(a) $x^2 - x = 69$ (b) $x^2 + 3x = 43$ (c) $x(x - 4) = 27$

2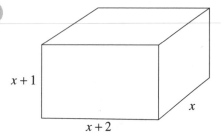

The volume of this cuboid is 143 cm³. Use trial and improvement to find the value of x, correct to 1 decimal place.

3 Solve the equation $5^x = 66$, giving your answer correct to 1 decimal place.

4 The shaded area shown opposite is 419 cm². Use trial and improvement to find the value of x, correct to 1 decimal place.

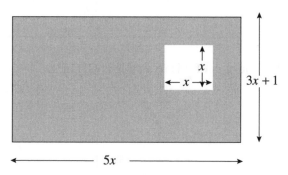

4.3 Finding a rule

1 Look at the sequence and the table underneath. Find the nth term of each sequence.

(a) Sequence 4, 11, 18, 25, ...

n	$7n$	term
1	7	4
2	14	11
3	21	18
4	28	25

n^{th} term = ☐

(b) Sequence 1, 5, 9, 13, ...

n	$4n$	term
1	4	1
2	8	5
3	12	9
4	16	13

n^{th} term = ☐

2 Look at the sequence 7, 10, 13, 16, ...

Write down the diference between terms. Make a table like the one in question **1** and use it to find an expression for the nth term.

3 Below you are given a sequence in a table. Copy the table and make an extra column. Find an expression for the nth term of each sequence. (t stands for 'term')

(a)
n	t
1	7
2	9
3	11
4	13
5	15

(b)
n	t
1	5
2	11
3	17
4	23
5	29

(c)
n	t
1	8
2	13
3	18
4	23
5	28

(d)
n	t
1	3
2	12
3	21
4	30
5	39

(e)
n	t
1	9
2	17
3	25
4	33
5	41

4 Write down each sequence in a table and then find the nth term.

(a) 3, 13, 23, 33, ...   (b) 9, 13, 17, 21, ...   (c) 5, 13, 21, 29, ...

5 Find the nth term of each sequence below:

(a) 11, 17, 23, 29, ...   (b) 1, 6, 11, 16, ...   (c) 17, 14, 11, 8, ...

HWK 1E ————————————————————— **Main Book Page 165**

1 Here is a sequence of shapes made from a number of matches m.

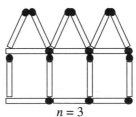

n = 1   n = 2   n = 3
m = 6   m = 11   m = 16

n	m
1	6
2	11
3	16
4	

Draw the next diagram in the sequence and write the values for n and m in a table. How many matches are in the nth term?

2 Repeat question **1** for the sequence of shapes shown below.

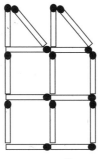
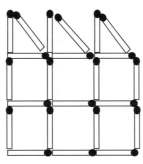

n = 1   n = 2   n = 3

70

3 Pam is putting up a fence. Each extra section is added as shown below, n stands for the number of sections.

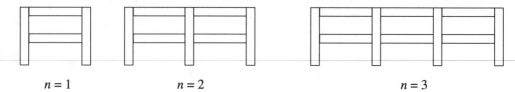

n = 1   n = 2   n = 3

(a) Complete the table where p is how many pieces of wood are used.
(b) Find an expression for how many pieces of wood are used for n sections of the fence.
(c) How many pieces of wood are used for 24 sections of the fence?

n	p
1	4
2	
3	
4	

4 Shapes are drawn on rectangular 'dotty' paper. The diagram number of the shape is recorded together with the total number of dots d on each shape.

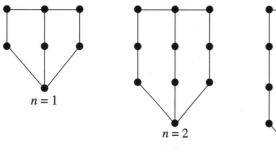

n = 1

n = 2

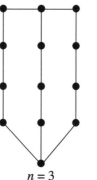

n = 3

n	d
1	7
2	
3	
4	

How many dots are there on the nth shape in the sequence?

5 Martin is given £80 on his birthday. He decides to save the money. Each week after his birthday he saves a further £7. How much has he got saved after:

(a) 2 weeks?   (b) 3 weeks?   (c) 4 weeks?   (d) 5 weeks?

(e) Write down an expression for how much he has got saved after n weeks.

(f) How much has he got saved after 20 weeks?

(g) How much has he got saved after one year?

(h) After how many weeks will he have saved £255?

HWK 2M ──────────────────────────── **Main Book Page 167**

1 The terms of a quadratic sequence are given by n^{th} term $= n^2 + 3n - 2$.

$n = 1$ gives the 1st term $= 1^2 + (3 \times 1) - 2 = 1 + 3 - 2 = 2$

$n = 2$ gives the 2nd term $= 2^2 + (3 \times 2) - 2 = 4 + 6 - 2 = 8$

Work out (a) 3rd term

   (b) 4th term

   (c) 5th term

2 n^{th} term $= n^2 + 7n + 1$. Write down the first 5 terms of this sequence.

3 Use each formula to find the first 6 terms of a quadratic sequence.

(a) n^{th} term $= n^2 + 9$ (b) n^{th} term $= n^2 + 5n - 4$

(c) n^{th} term $= n^2 + 8n + 3$ (d) n^{th} term $= 4n^2 + n$

4 (a) n^{th} term $= n^2 + 6n - 3$. Write down the first six terms of this sequence.

(b) Write down the difference between each pair of terms. What pattern do you notice?

HWK 2E ──────────────────────────── **Main Book Page 168**

> Remember for quadratic sequences:
>
> n^{th} term formula contains $2n^2$ if second difference $= 4$
>
> n^{th} term formula contains $3n^2$ if second difference $= 6$

Use second differences to help you find the nth term of these sequences.

1 5, 11, 21, 35, 53, ….. **2** 2, 11, 26, 47, 74, …

3 8, 11, 16, 23, 32, … **4** −1, 5, 15, 29, 47, …

5 2, 14, 34, 62, 98, ... **6** 6, 21, 46, 81, 126, ...

7 6, 24, 54, 96, 150, ... **8** 9, 21, 41, 69, 105, ...

9 2, 6, 12, 20, 30, ... **10** 1, 5, 11, 19, 29, ...

4.4 Averages and range

1 Which set of numbers below has the larger range?

Set A	9	5	13	3	17	4	5	12	8

Set B	6	14	8	19	9	7	18	9	13	11

2 Write down the median of the list of numbers below:

$$-2, \quad -6, \quad 0, \quad -8, \quad 6, \quad -4, \quad 4, \quad -2, \quad -5$$

3 Explain how you find the mode of a list of numbers.

4

Set P	
12	18
15	12
17	16
13	13
10	

Which set of numbers has the larger mean and by how much?

Set Q	
21	22
12	13
16	11
9	9
10	12

5 The stem and leaf diagram shows the ages of 23 people in a cinema.

(a) What is the median age?

(b) Write down the range of the ages.

Stem	Leaf
1	4 6 6 7
2	1 1 3 5 5 8
3	0 2 4 8
4	1 5 5 9 9
5	4
6	2 7 7

4|5 means 45

6 Ann, Michael and Sasha are given an 8 week trial to sell computers. One person will then be given a job at the end of this time period. The number of computers they sell each week is shown below:

Week		1	2	3	4	5	6	7	8
number of computers sold.	Ann	4	6	1	7	3	6	7	6
	Sasha	7	9	3	5	7	4	8	5
	Michael	10	6	2	12	2	10	1	5

(a) Find the mean and range for each person.

(b) The job is given to the person who sells the most computers but is also the most *consistent* seller. Who gets the job? *Explain why.*

7 The two stem and leaf diagrams show the marks for children from two classes who sat a maths exam.

Class 9A	Stem	Leaf
	4	3 3 5
	5	0 1 1 6 8
	6	1 2 2 4 6 9
	7	3 4 4 8 8 9
	8	2 5 6 6 8
	9	0 2 7 7 9

Class 9B	Stem	Leaf
	3	6 9
	4	2 2 5 6 7
	5	3 3 6 8 9 9
	6	4 6 7 7
	7	0 3 8 8
	8	4 4 6 7 9
	9	2 7

Key 7|4 = 74%

(a) Which class had the higher median mark?

(b) In which class were the marks spread out less widely?

HWK 1E — **Main Book Page 172**

1 The mean weight of 5 people is 68 kg. One person leaves the group. The mean weight of the remaining 4 people is 70 kg. How much did the person who left the group weigh?

2 Fran has 5 cards. The 5 cards have a mean of 7 and a range of 12. What numbers belong on the other two cards?   6   7   8   ☐   ☐

3 The weights of the pack players in two rugby teams is shown below. The weights are in kg.

Team A	101	96	98	103	101	92	105	96
Team B	99	97	103	94	108	x	98	102

If the mean pack weight is the same for both teams, calculate the missing weight for team B.

4 Terry does 3 spelling tests. The mean test mark is 15 and his median test mark is 14. What are the other two test results if the range is 7?

5 The number of people attending a nightclub each Saturday night is shown below for a run of 16 Saturdays.

Stem	Leaf
14	. . . .
15	. . . .
..	. . . .
..	. . . .

148   163   161   179   142   153   148   164

173   154   164   158   175   146   163   147

(a) Draw an ordered stem and leaf diagram.

(b) Find the median for this data.

6 The mean amount of weekly pocket money received by a group of 19 children is £7. Another child joins the group. She receives £11 pocket money each week. What is now the mean amount of weekly pocket money received by the group of 20 children?

7 This back-to-back stem and leaf diagram shows the ages of people in two pubs on one particular night.

The Crown		The Mitre
9 9 9 9 8 8 8	1	8 8 9
9 9 8 6 3 3 3 2	2	0 1 1 1 4 7 8
8 8 5 5 4 0	3	2 2 5 7 8 9
7 6 6 3 1	4	3 7 7
4 2	5	4 8 9 9
	6	2 6
	7	3 4

$4|5 = 54$ $3|7 = 37$

(a) Find the range and median age for The Mitre.

(b) Find the range and median age for The Crown.

(c) Write a sentence to compare the ages of the people in the two pubs.

HWK 2M ────────────────────────── **Main Book Page 174**

1 The table below shows the number of pets owned by 50 families.

number of pets	0	1	2	3	4	5	6	7
frequency	14	9	12	4	5	2	3	1

Copy and complete:

mean number of pets $= \dfrac{(14 \times 0) + (9 \times 1) + (12 \times 2) + ...}{50}$

$= \dfrac{\square}{50} = \square$

2 The table below shows the number of pencils in 20 different pencil cases.

number of pencils	1	2	3	4	5	6	7	8
frequency	2	4	1	5	3	2	1	2

Calculate the mean number of pencils in each pencil case.

3 25 people were asked how often they had filled their car with petrol during the previous fortnight. The results are shown in the table below.

number of fills	0	1	2	3	4	5	6
frequency	1	3	7	5	4	2	3

Find   (a) the mean number of fills

(b) the modal number of fills (this means the 'mode', ie. the most common number of fills)

4

number of holidays abroad	frequency
0	42
1	29
2	46
3	53
4	28
5	32
6	9
7	11

This table shows how many holidays abroad were taken by 250 people over the last 3 years.

Find

(a) the mean number of holidays

(b) the modal number of holidays

4 Some bags of flour in a shop were weighed. The table below shows the results. Calculate the mean weight of the bags of flour.

weight (g)	497	498	499	500	501	502
number of bags	2	7	17	36	33	5

HWK 2E   **Main Book Page 176**

1 The weights of 40 people were measured and are shown in the table.

Weight (kg)	Mid-point	Frequency
40–50	45	7
50–60	55	13
60–70	65	8
70–80	75	7
80–90	85	5

(a) Copy and complete:

$$\text{mean weight} = \frac{(7 \times 45) + (13 \times 55) + (8 \times 65) + ...}{40}$$

$$= \frac{\square}{40} = \square \text{ kg}$$

(b) *Explain* why your answer is only an *estimate* of the mean weight.

2 Calculate an estimate for the mean for the information shown in each table.

(a)

Height (cm)	Mid-point	Frequency
110–120	115	8
120–130		19
130–140		14
140–150		6
150–160		3

(b)

Length (m)	Mid-point	Frequency
0–0.5	0.25	3
0.5–1		1
1–1.5		7
1.5–2		3
2–2.5		4
2.5–3		2

3 The times taken by runners in a 1500 m race are recorded in this table.

Calculate an estimate for the mean time taken by the runners.

Time (s)	Mid-point	Frequency
225–230		1
230–235		3
235–240		6
240–245		7
245–250		2
250–255		1

4.5 Ratio and map scales

HWK 1M ——————————————————————— **Main Book Page 178**

A train carriage has 10 windows and 12 wheels.

Each window has handles.

(Number of handles: number of windows = 3:1)

An engine is put on the front and end of each row of carriages.

(Number of engines: number of carriages = 2:7)

1 How many carriages are used with:

(a) 4 engines?   (b) 8 engines?   (c) 10 engines?

2 How many engines are used with:

(a) 21 carriages?   (b) 49 carriages?   (c) 63 carriages?

3 How many windows will have 15 handles?

4 How many carriages have 84 wheels?

5 The carriages on same trains have 140 windows in total. How many engines are used?

6 Six engines are used on some trains. What is the total number of wheels on the carriages used on these trains?

7 Seventeen handles on the windows of six carriages are damaged. How many handles on these carriages are not damaged?

HWK 1E ———————————————————————— **Main Book Page 179**

Remember: 15:9 can be simplified to 5:3

Write these ratios in a more simple form.

1. 8:4
2. 3:12
3. 8:30
4. 12:9
5. 5:45
6. 10:25
7. 15:12
8. 14:21
9. 50:35
10. 7:42
11. 16:24
12. 32:24
13. 80:36
14. 49:28
15. 11:55
16. 72:81
17. 3:12:18
18. 5:30:55
19. 99:63:18
20. 14:56:35
21. 30:75:120
22. 36:96:48
23. 40:100:80
24. 51:85:68

HWK 2M ———————————————————————— **Main Book Page 180**

Share these quantities in the ratios given.

1. 20 pens between Alice and Ryan, ratio 1:3
2. 42 magazines between Mo and Carl, ratio 4:3
3. 27 chocolates between Charlie and Pippa, ratio 2:7
4. 56 sweets between Peta and Tamsin, ratio 6:1
5. 48 apples between Naomi and Richard, ratio 3:5
6. 45 loaves of bread between Dan, Jane and Tariq, ratio 3:2:4
7. 78 oranges between Shane, Annie and Emily, ratio 2:5:6
8. 64 cd's between Tom, Rita and John, ratio 8:3:5
9. £132 is shared in the ratio 5:6. What is the largest share worth?
10. £126 is shared in the ratio 8:3:7. What is the smallest share worth?

HWK 2E ———————————————————————— **Main Book Page 180**

1. In a restaurant, the ratio of knives to forks is 6:5. There are 210 forks. How many knives are there?
2. The ratio of boys to girls in a classroom is 4:3. How many children are there in total if there are 20 boys?
3. Write down the ratio of (shaded area): (white area) for this shape.

4 The ratio of beer to lemonade in a shandy drink is 3:2. How much beer is used with 6 litres of lemonade?

5 A scarf is made from blue and yellow stripes. $\frac{4}{7}$ of the scarf is blue. What is the ratio of blue to yellow?

6 Gin and tonic is mixed in the ratio 2:5. How much tonic will be mixed with 80 ml of gin?

7 £22750 is shared between Gerald, Vicky, Caroline and Andy in the ratio 11:15:7:2. How much does each person get?

8

Write down the following ratios:

(a) area A: area C

(b) area B: area C

(c) area C: area B

2 cm

3 cm

1 cm A

B

C

1 cm

2 cm

3 cm

9 Darren and Max work in a circus. They are paid in the ratio of their heights. Darren is 2m tall and Max is 1.6 m tall. How much is Max paid if Darren is paid £360 each week?

10 The employees in a firm either work in the office, sell or work in the factory. They do this in the ratio 5:6:29. How many employees are there in total if 42 people sell?

HWK 3M/3E — **Main Book Page 182**

1 Two villages are 3 cm apart on a map whose scale is 1:200 000. Find the actual distance (in km) between the two villages.

2 A map with a scale of 1:40000 shows that one side of a park is 2.5 cm long. What is the actual length of this side of the park?

3 A road is 25 cm long on a map whose scale is 1:100 000. Find the actual length of the road.

4

Corley

10 km

14 km

Halby

7 km

Henton

These villages are marked on a map with a scale of 1:200 000.

What is the length on the map:

(a) from Henton to Halby?

(b) from Halby to Corley?

(c) from Corley to Henton?

5 The length of a playing field is 90 m. How long will this be on a map with a scale of 1:4000?

6 A ship sails from one port to another. Its journey is 15.6 cm long on a map. How long is the actual journey if the map scale is 1:5000 000?

7 Copy and complete this table.

Map scale	Actual length on land	Length on map
(a) 1:80 000	6 km	cm
(b) 1:30 000	15 km	cm
(c) 1:4000 000	260 km	cm

8 The scale of the plan of a house is 1 cm to 1.5 m. The height of the house is 16.5 m. What will the height of the house be on the plan?

9 The rectangular field opposite is drawn on a map with a scale of 1:5000.

What is the actual area of this field?

1.8 cm

4.4 cm

10 Mia is planning a walk. She has to use two maps. She wants to walk from Garby to Hendleford then from Hendleford to Wendon. The first map with a scale of 1:20 000 shows the distance from Garby to Hendleford is 35 cm. The second map with a scale of 1:50 000 shows the distance from Hendleford to Wendon is 11 cm. What will be the actual total distance of Mia's walk from Gardy to Wendon?

4.6 Locus

HWK 1M/1E   **Main Book Page 185**

1
```
A      4 cm      B
 ┌─────────────┐
 │             │
3 cm           │
 │             │
 └─────────────┘
D               C
```
Draw this rectangle accurately. Shade an area inside the rectangle to show all the points which are less than or equal to 2 cm from the corner A.

2 Draw any two pionts P and Q. Draw the locus of all the points which are equidistant from P and Q. ('equidistant' means an equal distance, ie. the same length)

3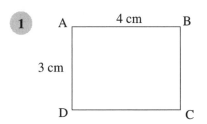

Draw three rectangles like this with a scale of 1 cm to 1 m. Use a different rectangle to draw each of the following loci:
(a) Points in the room equidistant from P and S.
(b) Points in the room which are more than or equal to 3 m from R.
(c) Points in the room which are equidistant from the lines PS and SR.

80

4 (a) Draw the places opposite using a scale of 1 cm to 5 km.

(b) Jacqui lives within 20 km of Benford and within 15 km of Chowley. On your diagram show the area where Jacqui might live.

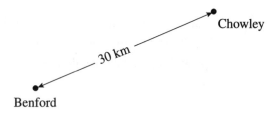

5 Draw a line AB of length 6 cm. Draw the locus of all the points which are 3 cm from the line AB.

6 (a) Draw the diagram opposite using a scale of 1 cm to 20 m.

(b) A pipe is to be laid which is equidistant from A and B as well as being within 90 m of B. Show clearly exactly where the pipe is to be laid.

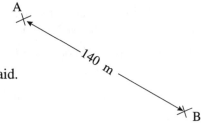

7

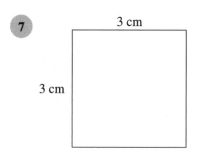

Draw this square accurately. Draw the locus of all the points which are exactly 1 cm from the edge of the square and outside the square.

4.7 Fully functional 2

HWK 1M/2M ———————————————— **Main Book Page 189**

Phil is trying to start his own business. He is producing resource packs about different countries which he wants to sell to schools, particularly nursery schools.

His costs and selling prices are shown below:

resource pack name	cost of raw materials (£)
Greece	2.46
Spain	2.73
India	4.15
U.S.A.	2.45
Australia	2.25
China	4.04
France	2.49

Phil must market his packs if he wants to sell as many as possible. Every 2 weeks he spends £83 on marketing.

resource pack name	pack selling price (£)
Greece	7
Spain	7
India	9.50
U.S.A.	6.50
Australia	6
China	9.50
France	7

Phil must pay insurance in case his packs lead to any accidents. This costs him £18.75 each week.

Phil works from home. The extra gas/electricity used costs him £15 weekly

Profit from postage and package

Phil posts the packs to schools and charges extra for postage and package.

- if he sends 1 pack only, he makes £1.20 profit

- if he sends 2 packs together, he makes £1.60 profit

- if he sends 3 packs together, he makes £2 profit

Task

Once Phil's business is up and running, the number of sales of each pack during the first 4 weeks is shown below.

resource pack name	week 1	week 2	week 3	week 4
Greece	3	2	4	7
Spain	1	5	7	6
India	0	6	10	12
U.S.A.	1	3	5	6
Australia	2	7	3	5
China	1	6	10	15
France	0	4	6	5

The number of packs sent out together each week is shown below.

week 1	5 × 1 pack, 1 × 3 packs
week 2	4 × 1 pack, 7 × 2 packs, 5 × 3 packs
week 3	9 × 1 pack, 9 × 2 packs, 6 × 3 packs
week 4	15 × 1 pack, 10 × 2 packs, 7 × 3 packs

1 Phil wants to make £140 profit per week on average during these 4 weeks. Does he manage this? you must show all your working out. Remember the money he makes from the postage and package.

2 Does the sales pattern suggest that Phil's business will be successful in the long term? *Explain* your reasons for giving your answer.

UNIT 5

5.1 Pythagoras' theorem

HWK 1M ——————————————————————————— **Main Book Page 207**

Remember:

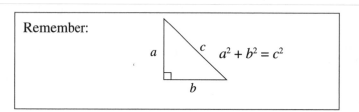

$a^2 + b^2 = c^2$

You will need a calculator. The units are cm. Give your answers to 2 decimal places where necessary.

1 Find the side marked with a letter. It may be the hypotenuse or one of the other sides.

(a)

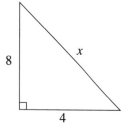

(b)

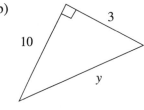

(c)

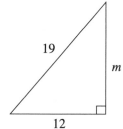

(d)

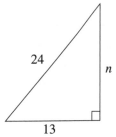

(e)

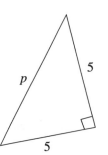

(f)

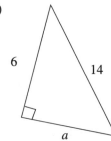

2 Find the side marked with a letter.

(a)

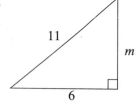

(b)

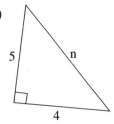

(c)

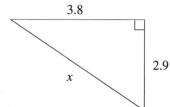

(d)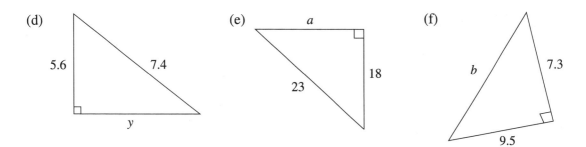

5.6   7.4

y

(e)   a

23   18

(f)

b   7.3

9.5

HWK 1E ——————————————— **Main Book Page 209**

You will need a calculator. Give your answers to 2 decimal places where necessary.

1 A balloon flies 20 miles due north and then a further 12 miles due west. How far is the balloon from its starting point?

2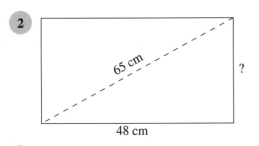

65 cm

48 cm

?

The diagonal for this TV screen is 65 cm. Find the height of this TV screen.

3 A ladder of length 4.5 m rests against a vertical wall, with its foot 1.9 m from the wall. How far up the wall does the ladder reach?

4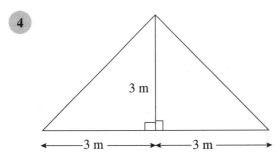

3 m

—3 m— —3 m—

Part of a building is made from metal rods as shown opposite. Calculate the total length of all the metal rods.

5 Calculate the length BD in the diagram opposite.

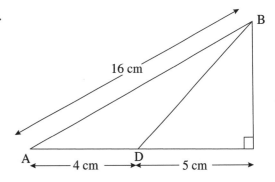

B

16 cm

A — 4 cm — D — 5 cm —

6 Ian walks 9 km due south then 8 km due east. He then walks directly back to his starting point. How far does he walk in total?

7 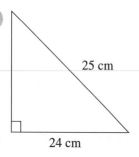 Calculate the area of this triangle.

25 cm

24 cm

8 Explain why this triangle is not right-angled.

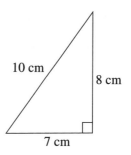

10 cm

8 cm

7 cm

9 (a) Calculate the height of this isosceles triangle.

(b) Calculate the area of this isosceles triangle.

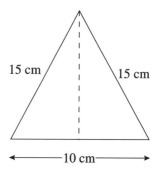

15 cm

15 cm

10 cm

5.2 Number Review

HWK 1M ——————————————————— **Main Book Page 211**

Work out

1 $760 \div 100$ **2** $5.6 + 3$ **3** 0.3×100 **4** $3.1 - 0.96$

5 $724 \div 10$ **6** £7.87 + £3.50   **7** 5.12×10 **8** $6 \div 10$

9 £4658 was shared equally between 34 people. How much did each person receive?

10 Work out

(a) $476 \div 17$ (b) 536×46 (c) 279×68 (d) $9288 \div 43$

11 A rugby shirt costs £42.99. A rugby team manager must buy 24 shirts. Work out the total cost.

12 Work out

    (a) $0.7 + 0.03$ (b) $8 - 2.3$ (c) $0.42 \div 7$ (d) 0.8^2

13 Find the cost of 8 magazines at £3.79 each and 5 books at £7.99 each.

14 How many 0.005 litre doses can be taken from a 0.2 litre bottle of medicine?

15 Write 'one million and forty' in figures.

HWK 1E   **Main Book Page 212**

1 Work out

    (a) $7 - (-3)$ (b) $6 \times (-8)$ (c) $(-10) \div (-5)$ (d) $-8 + 6$

    (e) $(-7) \times (-4)$ (f) $-5 - 8$ (g) $(-5)^2$ (h) $(-20) \div 4$

    (i) $4 \times (-3)^2$ (j) $-9 + 7$ (k) $(-3) \times (-8)$ (l) $35 \div (-7)$

    (m) $(-36) \div (-9)$ (n) $-16 - (-4)$ (o) $(-6) \times 9$ (p) $(-8)^2$

2 Which question below gives the largest answer?

    A $\boxed{(-3) \times (-2)}$ B $\boxed{(-2)^2}$ C $\boxed{8 \times (-3)}$ D $\boxed{-6 + 11}$ E $\boxed{4 \times (-1)^2}$

3 Work out

    (a) $\frac{1}{2} \times (-6)$ (b) $\left(\frac{-1}{4}\right) \times 12$ (c) $5 \div \left(\frac{-1}{2}\right)$ (d) $-1 - \left(\frac{-1}{2}\right)$

4 Find the value of

    $-8 + (-3) + 10 - 4 - (-7) - 2$

5 Which question below gives the odd answer out?

    P $\boxed{(-3)^2 - 10}$ Q $\boxed{(-24) \div (-4)}$ R $\boxed{3 - 9 - (-5)}$

6 Find the value of

    $(-8) \times (-7) - (-2) \times 3$

HWK 2M   **Main Book Page 213**

1 Work out

    (a) $\frac{2}{5} + \frac{1}{3}$ (b) $\frac{7}{8} - \frac{4}{7}$ (c) $\frac{4}{9} - \frac{3}{10}$ (d) $\frac{2}{11} + \frac{3}{4}$

2 Jennifer has collected 340 different badges. 68 of these badges involve sport.
    What percentage of the badges do *not* involve sport?

3 Spot the dog weighs 18 kg. Spot loses 5% of his weight during an illness. How much does Spot now weigh?

4 Work out

(a) $\frac{3}{5}$ of 60

(b) $\frac{6}{7}$ of 56

(c) $\frac{4}{5} \times \frac{15}{16}$

(d) $\frac{7}{10} \times \frac{2}{3}$

5 A plant costs £3.90. Tyrone gets a 6% discount if he buys 45 plants. How much will he pay in total for the 45 plants?

6 Which question below gives the odd answer out?

A $\boxed{35\% \text{ of } 1200}$ B $\boxed{16\% \text{ of } 2400}$ C $\boxed{60\% \text{ of } 700}$

7 Trevor is interested in buying one of two cars. The Corsa is priced at £7500 and the Galant costs £8600. Trevor is offered a 15% discount on the Corsa and a 25% discount on the Galant. Which car is cheaper and by how much?

8 Work out

(a) $\frac{2}{5} \div \frac{5}{8}$

(b) $\frac{4}{9} \div \frac{3}{4}$

(c) $\frac{3}{8} \div \frac{9}{10}$

(d) $\frac{2}{7} \div \frac{4}{5}$

HWK 2E ————————————————————— **Main Book Page 214**

1 Work out

(a) $1\frac{1}{2} + 2\frac{2}{3}$

(b) $4\frac{3}{5} - 1\frac{9}{10}$

(c) $3\frac{1}{4} - 1\frac{5}{7}$

2 Rosie buys a car for £9100 and sells it two year later for £4095. Calculate the percentage loss.

3 Kevin has put on a little weight and now weighs 81.12kg. This is a 4% gain in weight. What did Kevin weigh before?

4 Work out

(a) $1\frac{2}{5} \times \frac{5}{8}$

(b) $2\frac{1}{3} \times \frac{9}{10}$

(c) $3\frac{1}{2} \times 1\frac{1}{3}$

5 A shop puts its prices up by 12%. A computer game now costs £47.04. How much did the computer game cost before the increase?

6 The monthly Gym membership increases from £24 to £25.44. What is the percentage increase?

7 Work out

(a) $2\frac{3}{4} \div 2\frac{1}{2}$

(b) $3\frac{1}{2} \div 1\frac{3}{4}$

(c) $1\frac{2}{3} \div 2\frac{1}{3}$

8 A dvd player costs £91.65 including VAT at 17.5%. What was the cost of the dvd player before the VAT was added?

HWK 3M ──────────────────────────── **Main Book Page 215**

Do not use a calculator.

1 Decimals. Work out

(a) $8 - 4.3$　　　　(b) 15×0.4　　　　(c) $2.86 \div 0.1$　　　　(d) 10×0.67

(e) $7 + 3.6$　　　　(f) $0.3 \div 0.1$　　　　(g) $6.76 \div 0.2$　　　　(h) 78×0.03

2 Estimation. Estimate the answer

(a) 31.2×5.08　　　(b) $796.3 \div 38.9$　　　(c) $203 \div 40.37$　　　(d) $\dfrac{3.9^2 + 8.04^2}{9.97}$

3 Order of operations. Work out

(a) $20 - 3 \times 2$　　　(b) $10 + 10 \div 2$　　　(c) $(8 \times 6) \div 16$　　　(d) $13 - (9 - 4)$

(e) $8 \times 2 + 3 \times 5$　　(f) $4^2 + 5 \times 6$　　(g) $27 - (4^2 + 3)$　　(h) $6 \times 7 - 12 \div 3$

4 Miscellaneous.

(a) List all the factors of 48.

(b) Decrease £480 by $2\frac{1}{2}\%$.

(c) Add together all the prime numbers shown opposite.

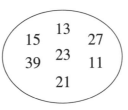

(d) Put the answers to the questions below in order of size, starting with the smallest.

P　$\boxed{0.7 \times 0.4}$　　　Q　$\boxed{0.5 \div 2}$　　　R　$\boxed{3.74 - 3.48}$　　　S　$\boxed{0.6^2}$

(e) What is the Lowest Common Multiple of 16 and 10?

HWK 3E ──────────────────────────── **Main Book Page 216**

Do not use a calculator.

1 Ryan works in a tea shop. He is paid £5.40 per hour. He is paid time and a half for working on a Sunday. On Friday he works for 7 hours and he works for 6 hours on Sunday. How much does he earn in total for this work?

2 What is the perimeter of this isosceles triangle (in centimetres)?

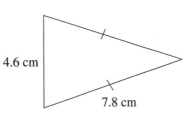

3 Work out

(a) 318×67 (b) $1092 \div 28$ (c) $1692 \div 47$ (d) 57^2

4 Write down the number half way between 17.4 and 17.5.

5 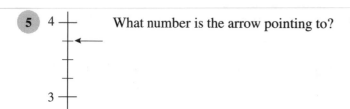 What number is the arrow pointing to?

6 A bag contains 2 kg of flour. Michelle uses 635 g of flour from the bag. How much flour is left in the bag?

7

Bristol	13:12
Bath	13:25
Reading	14:04
London	14:49

This table shows part of a train timetable.

(a) How long does it take to get from Bristol to Reading?

(b) William arrives at the train station in Bristol at 12:35. The train to London is 17 minutes late arriving. How long does William have to wait in total for the London train to arrive?

8 Put brackets in the correct position to make this calculation work.

$$24 - 12 - 9 \times 3 = 15$$

9 What percentage of these ticks and crosses are ticks?

   ✓ ✗ ✗ ✗ ✓

   ✗ ✓ ✗ ✓ ✗

   ✗ ✗ ✗ ✓ ✓

   ✓ ✗ ✗ ✗ ✗

10 Copy and complete these calculations.

(a) $100 \times \boxed{} = 46$ (b) $240 \div \boxed{} = 15$ (c) $5\% \text{ of } \boxed{} = 7.5$

(d) $\boxed{} - 6.3 = 8.14$ (e) $\frac{4}{5} \text{ of } \boxed{} = 36$ (f) $\boxed{} \times 0.8 = 0.032$

5.3 Probability

1 | 5 | | 7 | | 7 | | 9 | | 9 | | 9 | | 11 |

One card is picked at random from the cards shown above.

Find the probability that it is

(a) a multiple of 3

(b) more than 7

(c) a prime number

2 A bag contains red, yellow and green balls as
shown opposite.

(a) Find the probability of selecting a yellow ball?

(b) Six more red balls are added to the bag.
Find the probability of selecting a green ball.

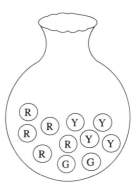

3 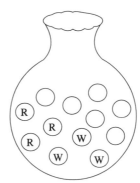   One card is picked at random from the cards shown opposite.
Find the probability that it is

(a) a '✓'

(b) not a 'O'

(c) a '✗' or a 'O'

4

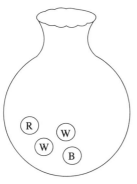

Gemma's bag   Mark's bag

Gemma and Mark each have a bag of balls which are red, white or blue.

(a) How many more of Mark's balls are white if he has the same probability of drawing
out a white ball as Gemma?

(b) How many of Mark's balls might be blue if he has less chance of drawing out a blue ball
than Gemma?

5

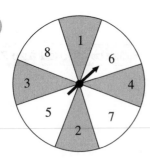

This spinner is spun 360 times. How often would you expect to get:

(a) an odd number?

(b) a multiple of 3?

(c) a square number?

HWK 2E ———————————————————————————————— **Main Book Page 223**

1 A shoe is thrown into the air. The probability of it landing 'heel down' is 63%.

(a) What is the probability of it not landing 'heel down'?

(b) How many times would you expect the shoe to land 'heel down' if it is thrown 400 times

2 The probability of throwing a double six with two dice is $\frac{1}{36}$. What is the probability of *not* throwing a double six?

3

A bag contains red and blue balls. The probability of picking a blue ball is $\frac{5}{9}$.

There are more than 10 balls in this bag.

Write down how many red balls could be in this bag?

4

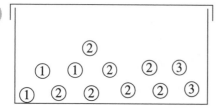

One number is selected at random from the box and then replaced. This is done 600 times. How many times would you expect to select:

(a) the number '1'?

(b) the number '2'?

5 A box contains 100 beads. There are *n* green beads and the remaining beads are yellow. Write down an expression for the probability of selecting a yellow bead.

6 Martin has a bag with 6 blue balls and 1 green ball. He says the probability of taking out a green ball is $\frac{1}{6}$.

Is he correct? Give a reason for your answer.

7 Emma spins the spinner and throws the dice.
She might get a 'B' and a '4', ie. B4.

(a) List all the possible outcomes.

(b) What is the probability of getting a 'C'
with an even number?

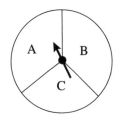

8 List all the ways of arranging the 3 letters $\boxed{A}$, $\boxed{B}$ and $\boxed{C}$. For example, CAB.
How many different ways did you find?

HWK 3M ———————————————————— **Main Book Page 224**

1 The probability of Kate having a cup of tea in the morning is $\frac{9}{10}$. What is the probability
of Kate not having a cup of tea in the morning?

2 Jake has only £20, £10 and £5 notes in his wallet. The next time he buys something, he uses
one of these notes.
The probability of using a £5 note is 0.1. The probability of using a £10 note is 0.5.
What is the probability that he uses a £20 note?

3 Wayne, Janice, Helen and Dom play a game of cards. The probability of each person winning
is shown in the table below.

Name	Wayne	Janice	Helen	Dom
Probability of winning	0.3	0.15	x	0.2

Find the probability of

(a) Janice or Don winning

(b) Helen winning

(c) Janice *not* winning

(d) How many times would you expect Wayne to win if they play 20 games?

4 A bag contains red, green, blue and yellow balls.
The table shows the probability of each colour
being drawn when one ball is removed from the bag.
What is the probability of drawing

(a) a green ball?

(b) a blue or yellow ball?

(c) *not* a blue ball?

red	0.35
green	n
blue	0.18
yellow	0.24

5 The probability of Hatton United winning their next football game is $\frac{2}{3}$.

The probability of Hatton United losing their next football game is $\frac{1}{4}$.

What is the probability of Hatton United drawing their next football game?

6 Sadie either walks, cycles or gets driven to school each morning.

The probability of walking is 0.38.

Sadie is twice as likely to walk as to cycle. What is the probability that Sadie will get driven to school?

7 The table below shows the probabilities of different types of animal being the next to arrive at an Animal Rescue Centre.

animal	cat	dog	rabbit	guinea pig	other
probability	$\frac{3}{10}$	$\frac{2}{5}$	x	$\frac{1}{10}$	$\frac{1}{20}$

Find the probability of the next animal being

(a) a cat or a dog

(b) a rabbit

(c) Out of the next 80 animals brought to the Animal Rescue Centre, how many would you expect to be dogs?

5.4 Interpreting graphs

HWK 1M ————————————————————— **Main Book Page 226**

1 The graph shows a car journey from Carlton to Wexford.

(a) For how long does the car stop in Dalby?

(b) How far is it from Dalby to Wexford?

(c) What is the speed of the car between Carlton and Dalby?

(d) The driver stops for petrol and takes a short break between Dalby and Wexford. For how long does the driver stop?

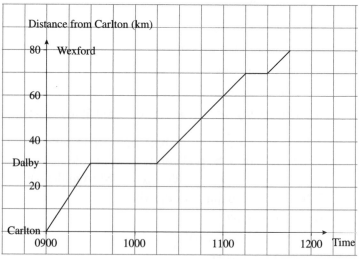

2

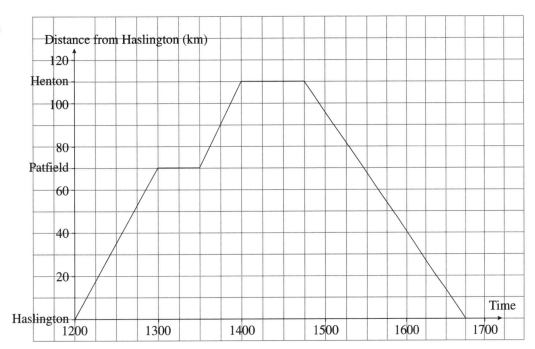

The graph above shows a car journey from Haslington to Henton and then back to Haslington.

(a) How far was the *total* journey?

(b) When did the car arrive back at Haslington?

(c) For how long did the car stop in Henton?

(d) Find the speed of the car

    (i) from Patfield to Henton   (ii) from Henton back to Haslington

3

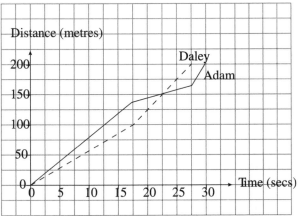

The graph above shows the performances of two runners during a 200 metres race.

(a) Who is winning after 10 seconds?

(b) At what time does Daley overtake Adam?

(c) Roughly how far behind Adam is Daley after 17.5 seconds?

(d) Who wins the race?

4

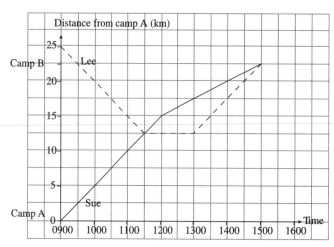

The graph above shows the walks of two hikers who start 25 km apart from each other.

(a) At what time do Lee and Sue first meet?

(b) For how long does Lee then stop for?

(c) How far ahead of Lee is Sue when Lee starts walking again?

(d) At what speed does Lee now walk in order to catch up with Sue?

HWK 1E   **Main Book Page 229**

1 (a) Draw a travel graph for the following journey.

'Tamsin leaves home at 1000.

She walks at 6 km/h for one hour then slows down to 4 km/h for the next $\frac{1}{2}$ hour. She stops for 15 minutes then walks for a further $1\frac{1}{2}$ hours at a speed of 6 km/h. She has then arrived at a lake.'

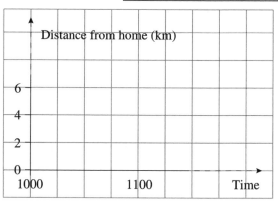

(b) Between what times did she stop for 15 minutes?

(c) At what time did she arrive at the lake?

(d) How far is the lake from Tamsin's home?

2 (a) Draw a travel graph for the following journey.

'Fergus leaves home at 1300. He travels at 80 km/h for 45 minutes then stops for $\frac{1}{2}$ hour. He then drives on a motorway for another $\frac{1}{2}$ hour at 120 km/h.

This gets him to an out of town shopping centre where he stays for one hour. He then travels directly home at a speed of 80 km/h.'

(b) At what time did he get to the shopping centre?

(c) How far is the shopping centre from his home?

(d) At what time did he get home?

3 (a) Write a short story like those in the last two questions which describe a journey.

   (b) Draw a travel graph to show this journey.

   (c) When you are back in class, get someone else to draw a travel graph for your story. Compare it to your travel graph.

1 The graph shows the amount of wine in a bottle during one evening. How many glasses of wine do you think were taken from the bottle?

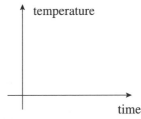

2 Which of the graphs A to D below best fits the following statement:
'The price of houses has been falling but increased slightly last month.

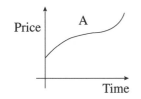 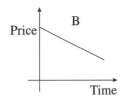 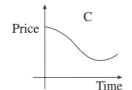 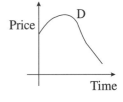

3 During the Summer, the temperature increases until the middle of the afternoon then it becomes cooler. Draw a sketch graph to show the temperature during the day.

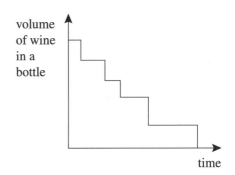

4 Water is poured into this container. Which of the graphs P to S below best shows how the water level would rise in the container?

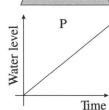 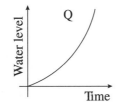 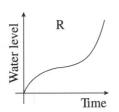 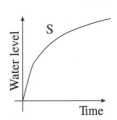

96

5 Tom saves money in a jar. He starts by putting £20 into the jar.
At the end of every month he puts another £5 into the jar.
Draw a sketch graph to show how much money is in the
jar during the first six months of saving.

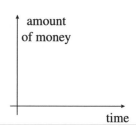

6 The graph opposite shows Amy's heart beat during one
part of the day. Describe what Amy could be doing to
produce this graph.

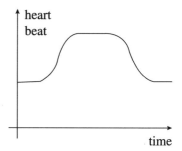

7 'The price of petrol has risen steadily over the last year but has stayed the same for the
last two months.' Sketch a graph to illustrate this statement.

8 'Over the last year the cost of holidays to Spain has increased steadily but has started to fall
over the last three months.' Sketch a graph to illustrate this statement.

9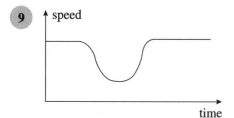

This graph shows the speed of a car during one part
of a race. Describe what might be happening during
this part of the race.

HWK 3M ——————————————————————— **Main Book Page 233**

1 Here is a frequency polygon showing the
heights of a group of young people.

(a) How many young people are there
in the group?

(b) How many people are more than
160 cm tall?

(c) What fraction of the people are
between 170 cm and 180 cm tall?

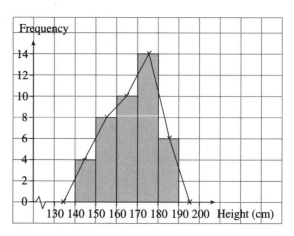

2. Draw a frequency polygon for the distribution of weights shown opposite for some dogs from a local kennels.

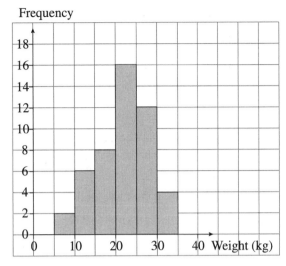

3.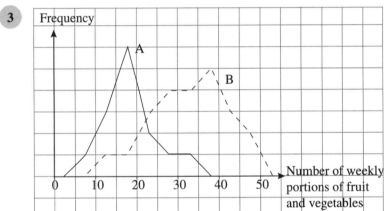

Two groups of people were asked how many portions of fruit and vegetables they ate last week. The results are shown in the frequency polygons above.

Describe the differences between the information shown for group A and group B. Which group of people do you think generally eat more healthily?

4. The weekly money earned by a group of sixteen year olds and a group of eighteen year olds for their holiday part-time jobs is shown in the tables opposite.

Using the same axes, with the money from £0 to £120, draw frequency polygons for the money earned by the sixteen year olds and for the money earned by the eighteen year olds.

Describe briefly the main differences between the two frequency polygons.

Sixteen year olds		Eighteen year olds	
money (£)	frequency	money (£)	frequency
10–20	2	40–50	1
20–30	5	50–60	2
30–40	8	60–70	4
40–50	9	70–80	5
50–60	6	80–90	9
60–70	1	90–100	7
		100–110	3

5.5 Compound Measures

HWK 1M ——————————————————————— **Main Book Page 236**

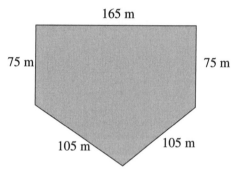

Remember: speed = $\dfrac{\text{distance}}{\text{time}}$

1 A car travels a distance of 300 m at a speed of 15 m/s. How long does it take?

2 A ship sails 168 km in 14 hours. How fast does it travel?

3 A man walks 0.8 km in 10 minutes. What is his speed in kilometres per hour?

4 A dog runs at a speed of 11.5 m/s. How far will the dog run in 6 seconds?

5 A coach travels at a speed of 76 km/h. How far does it travel in 2 hours 30 minutes?

6 A woman jogs around the edge of the park shown opposite. How long will it take her to jog around the edge of the park four times if her average speed is 3 m/s?

Give your answer in minutes and seconds.

165 m

75 m   75 m

105 m   105 m

7 A car travels 14 miles in 12 minutes. What is its speed in miles per hour?

8 A train travels at an average speed of 94 miles per hour. How far will it travel in 1 hour 15 minutes?

9 It takes 20 minutes for Stuart to cycle 7.2 km. How far does he travel in 2 hours?

10 Jack walks 28.8 km in 6 hours. Cheryl walks 1.24 km every 15 minutes. Who walks further in one hour and by how much?

HWK 1E ——————————————————————— **Main Book Page 237**

1 Find the time taken for the following:

(a)	2.5 miles at 10 mph
(b)	3 km at 50 m/s (note the units)
(c)	612 km at 18 km/h
(d)	2000 m at 8 km/h

2 A vehicle travels for 16s at a speed of 17 m/s. How far does it travel?

3 A sprinter covers 7 m in 0.8s. Find the sprinter's speed.

4 Penny walks at a speed of 6 km/h for 40 minutes. Darryl travels the same distance at a steady speed of 5 km/h. How long does Darryl walk for?

5 An astronomer is recording the path of a comet. The comet changes position by 92 km in 3 minutes. What is the speed of the comet in km/h?

6 Find the distance travelled using the information opposite.

(a)	3 cm/hour for 2 days
(b)	13 mph for 9 hours
(c)	20 m/s for 3 hours
(d)	4.5 m/s for 5 minutes

7 A ship sails at a speed of 12 knots for one day. How far does it travel?
(1 knot = 1 nautical mile per hour)

8 A train travels 315 km from London to York at an average speed of 175 km/h. When does the train arrive in York if it leaves London at 1315?

9 Jo and Maurice race against each other. Jo runs at 6 m/s and Maurice runs at 21 km/h. Who wins the race? You *must* show all your working out.

HWK 2M	Main Book Page 238

Remember: Density = $\dfrac{\text{Mass}}{\text{Volume}}$ Mass = Density × Volume

1 The mass of 45 cm³ of copper is 405 grams. What is the density of the copper?

2 The density of lead is 11.4 g/cm³. Calculate the weight of 300 cm³ of lead.

3 Find the volume of a piece of zinc which weighs 1308 g. The density of zinc is 6 g/cm³.

4 Copy and complete the table:

Density (g/cm³)	Mass (g)	Volume (cm³)
12		15
	56	7
8	192	
	3	0.5
5.6		20

5 The density of silk is 1.3 g/cm³. What is the mass of 9 cm³ of silk?

6 Which weighs more? 35 cm³ of iron with density 7.5 g/cm³ or 13 cm³ of gold with density 19 g/cm³.

7 If £1 = 1.15 euros,

    (a) change £750 into euros

    (b) change 69 euros into pounds

    (c) Anna buys a dress for 57.50 euros when on holiday in Spain. When she gets back to London, she finds the same dress on sale for £52. Which was the better deal – Spain or London? *Explain* why you make your choice.

8

| £1 = $1.45 (USA) | (a) Change 6475 yen into pounds. |
| £1 = 185 yen (Japan) | (b) Change £180 into dollars. |

    (c) Marie brings 13320 yen back from her holiday in Japan. Cornelius brings $98.60 back from his stay in New York. Who brings the most money back? *Explain* why you make your choice.

HWK 2E   **Main Book Page 239**

1 Some dress material costs £34 per metre. How much will 1.6 m cost?

2 26 m² of carpet costs £598. What is the cost per m² of the carpet?

3 Electrical cable costs £2.70 per metre.
What is the cost of buying this cable once completely around the edge of this room?

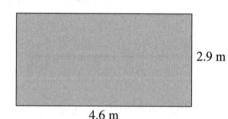

2.9 m

4.6 m

4 It costs £19 per minute to run an industrial machine. The machine runs all day except for two stoppages each of two hours duration. How much does it cost to run the machine for one complete seven day week?

5 A rectangular metal bar has dimensions 6 cm × 4 cm × 3 cm. Work out the weight of the metal bar if the metal density is 8 g/cm³.

6 A tile cutter is hired for 3 weeks. There is a fixed charge of £27 then a cost of £6.50 per day. How much will the hire of the tile cutter cost in total?

7

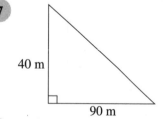

40 m

90 m

Raspberries are grown in this field. The farmer makes £2.25 per m². How much money will the farmer make in total?

8 A rock star earns 22p every second of the year. How much money does the rock star earn in one year?

5.6 Algebra Review

1 Answer true or false.

(a) $3 \times 5a = 35a$

(b) $8n \times 3n = 24n^2$

(c) $\dfrac{8m}{2} = 6m$

(d) $\dfrac{54x}{x} = 54$

(e) $5m \times n = 5mn$

(f) $\dfrac{36n}{4} = 9n$

Multiply out the expressions in questions **2** to **10**

2 $7(2m + 3)$

3 $8(4 + 5n)$

4 $3(9x - 4)$

5 $n(n + 7)$

6 $m(3 - 2n)$

7 $5(4p - 6q)$

8 $3m(4m + 2)$

9 $5p(4 - 3p)$

10 $8n(2m + n)$

11 Copy and complete:

$15 + 3n = 3(\square + n)$

> 3 is the common factor

Factorise the expressions in questions **12** to **20**, ie. take out the common factor first.

12 $4n + 6$

13 $24 + 14m$

14 $30 - 8x$

15 $7x + 21y$

16 $40m - 32n$

17 $16x - 12y + 10$

18 $30p - 15 + 10q$

19 $27m + 45n - 18r$

20 $35 + 14x - 42y$

1 Answer true or false

(a) $\dfrac{n + n}{2} = n$

(b) $n^3 \times n = n^3$

(c) $\dfrac{n^2}{n} = n$

(d) $\dfrac{m + m + m}{m} = 2m$

(e) $m + 2n - n - m = n$

(f) $\dfrac{n^2}{n^2} = 1$

Factorise the expressions in questions **2** to **10**

2 $4m^2 - 3m$

3 $a^2 + 5a$

4 $6n^2 + 2np$

5 $8xy - 6y$

6 $5mn + 10n$

7 $12abc - 6a^2$

8 $15n^2 - 3mn$

9 $24mnp + 18mp$

10 $20x^2 - 8xy$

In questions **11** to **18**, remove the brackets and simplify.

11 $5(x + 3) + 4x$

12 $7(3m + 2) - 6m$

13 $4(2n + 7) + 6(3n + 2)$

14 $6(5x + 1) + 3(2x + 9)$

15 $8(4x + 5) + 4(4 + 6x)$

16 $4(6m + 9) - 5(3m - 2)$

17 $7(5n + 3) - 5(6n - 8)$

18 $3(2m + 5) - 2(m + 4)$

HWK 2M | **Main Book Page 243**

1 Answer true or false

(a) $n^6 \times n^3 = n^{18}$

(b) $y^6 \div y^2 = y^4$

(c) $m^2 \times m^3 = m^5$

(d) $\dfrac{x^{10}}{x^5} = x^2$

(e) $p^6 \times p^2 = p^8$

(f) $\dfrac{n^8}{n^4} = n^4$

2 Here is a formula $y = 5x - 4$.

Find the value of y when

(a) $x = 6$

(b) $x = 15$

(c) $x = 1\frac{1}{2}$

3 Andreas hires a car. There is a fixed charge of £112 plus extra for each mile covered. The total cost C(£'s) is given by the formula

$$C = 112 + 0.14m$$

Where m is the number of miles travelled.

(a) Find C if $m = 320$.

(b) Find C if 465 miles are covered.

4 Simplify

(a) $\dfrac{n^7 \times n^3}{n^5}$

(b) $\dfrac{m^6 \times m^2}{m^3}$

(c) $\dfrac{n^5 \times n^3 \times n^4}{n^8}$

(d) $\dfrac{m^3 \times m^5 \times m^{10}}{m^9 \times m^4}$

(e) $\dfrac{a^8 \times a^4}{a^2 \times a^7}$

(f) $\dfrac{n^8 \times n^{12}}{n^3 \times n^7 \times n^3}$

5 (a) $m = 12n + 19$ Find m if $n = 8$.

(b) $p = \dfrac{8 + 2x}{10}$ Find p if $x = 16$.

(c) $y = n(4 + 3n)$ Find y if $n = 5$.

6

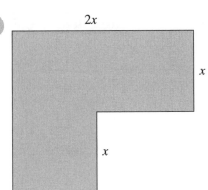

2x

x

x

x

The area A of this shape is given by the formula

$A = 3x^2$

(a) Find A if $x = 2$ (note the answer is *not* 36)

(b) Find A if $x = 10$

HWK 2E ———————————————— **Main Book Page 245**

Remember: $(a^m)^n = a^{mn}$

1 Answer true or false

(a) $(n^3)^5 = n^{15}$

(b) $4^0 = 0$

(c) $\dfrac{(m^3)^2}{m^2} = m^4$

(d) $\dfrac{m^0}{m^6} = \dfrac{1}{m^6}$

(e) $(x^4)^2 = x^6$

(f) $\dfrac{(n^5)^2}{n^7} = n^3$

2 The formula for the area A of a trapezium is

$A = \dfrac{1}{2} h(a + b)$

(a) Find A if $a = 6$, $b = 4$ and $h = 12$.

(b) Find A if $a = 3$, $b = 10$ and $h = 16$.

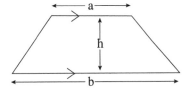

a

h

b

3 Simplify

(a) $\dfrac{(n^4)^3 \times n^5}{n^9}$

(b) $\dfrac{(m^7)^2 \times m^4}{(m^4)^2}$

(c) $\dfrac{n^0 \times (n^3)^3}{(n^2)^2}$

(d) $\dfrac{(m^6)^2 \times (m^3)^4}{(m^5)^4}$

(e) $\dfrac{a^{16}}{(a^3)^2 \times a^5}$

(f) $\dfrac{(m^4)^3 \times m^8}{m^4 \times (m^5)^2}$

4 (a) $y = ax + x^2$ Find y if $a = 4$ and $x = 3$.

(b) $m = n^2 + 5n - 3$ Find m if $n = 9$.

(c) $p = 5n^2 - 2n$ Find p if $n = 6$.

(d) $m = x(4x - 1)$ Find m if $x = 8$.

5 $s = ut + \dfrac{1}{2} at^2$ gives the distance from a fixed point of an object where u is its starting velocity, a is its acceleration and t is how long it has been travelling for.

Find the value of s when $t = 8$, $u = 43$ and $a = -10$.

104

1   (a) Copy and complete the table for $y = 3x - 5$

x	-2	-1	0	1	2	3	4
$3x$	-6						
-5	-5	-5					
y	-11						

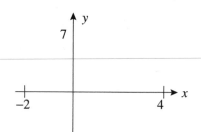

    (b) Draw the graph using the axes shown.

2   Draw the graph of $y = 5 - x$ for x-values from -2 to 5.

3   Draw the graph of $y = 2x - 1$ for x-values from -3 to 4.

4   (a) On the same graph, draw the lines

$$y = 2x + 4 \text{ and } y = 8 - 2x$$

     Take values of x from 0 to 5.

    (b) Write down the coordinates of the point of intersection of these two lines.

1   (a) Copy and complete the table for $y = x^2 - 2x$

x	-2	-1	0	1	2	3	4
x^2	4						16
$-2x$	4						-8
y	8						8

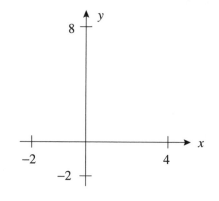

    (b) Draw the graph using the axes shown.

2   (a) Copy and complete the table for $y = x^2 + 2x - 3$

x	-4	-3	-2	-1	0	1	2
x^2	16					1	
$+2x$	-8					2	
-3	-3	-3				-3	
y	5					0	

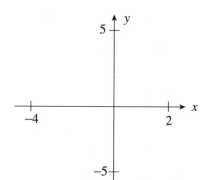

    (c) Draw the graph using the axes shown.

3   Draw the graph of $y = x^3 - x$ for x-values from -3 to 3.

HWK 4M ────────────────────────────── **Main Book Page 247**

1 We have the sequence

1, 8, 15, 22, …

The difference between terms is 7.

Look at the table which has a column for $7n$.

Write an expression for the nth term of the sequence.

n	$7n$	term
1	7	1
2	14	8
3	21	15
4	28	22

2 Find the nth term of each sequence below: (it may help to make tables like the table in question **1**)

(a) 5, 9, 13, 17, …   (b) 2, 10, 18, 26, …   (c) 8, 11, 14, 17, …   (d) 10, 27, 44, 61, …

3 Solve these equations

(a) $5x - 4 = 3x + 20$ (b) $33 = 8x + 9$ (c) $5(4x - 3) = 65$ (d) $7(x + 15) = 126$

(e) $4 + 6x = 10x - 32$ (f) $34 = 2(6x - 31)$

4 The nth term of a sequence is given by the formula

n^{th} term $= 3n + 7$

Find the value of n when the nth term $= 82$

5 If $m = 4n - 3$, find the value of n if $m = 57$.

6

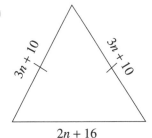

$3n + 10$ $3n + 10$

$2n + 16$

The perimeter of this triangle is 92 cm.

(a) Write down an equation involving n.

(b) Solve the equation to find n.

(c) Write down the length of each side of the triangle.

HWK 4E ────────────────────────────── **Main Book Page 247**

1 Use each formula to find the first 5 terms of a quadratic sequence.

(a) n^{th} term $= n^2 + 4$ (b) n^{th} term $= n^2 + 3n$

2 Use second differences to help you find the nth term of these sequences.

(a) 3, 6, 11, 18, 27, …   (b) 3, 12, 27, 48, 75, …   (c) 1, 7, 17, 31, 49, …

3 Solve the equations

   (a) $5x - 2 = 2$ (b) $9x + 7 = 6x + 6$ (c) $4(2x + 3) = 15$

   (d) $17 = 2(7 + x)$ (e) $3(5x - 2) = 7$ (f) $5(3x + 3) = 2(13 + 2x)$

4 Find the value of x for the rectangle shown opposite then write down the actual value of the perimeter. All lengths are in cm.

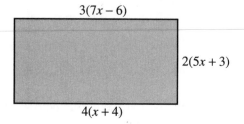

5 Use trial and improvement to find the length of this rectangular swimming pool if its length is 10 metres more than its width and its area is 278 m². Give the answer to one decimal place.

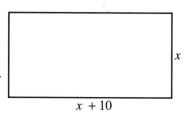

6 Use trial and improvement to solve the equation below, correct to one decimal place.

$$x^2 + 5x = 33$$

5.7 Errors in measurement

HWK 1M   **Main Book Page 249**

1 The diameter of a plate is 22 cm to the nearest cm. Write down the lower bound for the diameter of the plate.

2 Ann weighs 68 kg to the nearest kg. Write down the upper bound for Ann's weight.

3 The middle finger on Sam's left hand is measured at 7.3 cm to the nearest cm. What is the least possible length of Sam's middle finger?

4 Copy and complete the table below.
The first statement is done for you.

Quantity	Measured as:	Possible values
volume V	7 cm³ to the nearest cm³	$6.5 \leqslant V < 7.5$
width W	3.6 m to the nearest m	$\square \leqslant W < \square$
time T	8.9 s to the nearest s	$\square \leqslant T < \square$
height h	24 cm to the nearest cm	$\square \leqslant h < \square$
radius r	5.3 m to the nearest m	$\square \leqslant r < \square$

5 Mandy's suitcase weighs 4.7kg. Write down the lower and upper bounds for this weight.

6

9.4 cm

6.2 cm

The base and height of a triangle are measured to the nearest 0.1 cm, as shown.

(a) Write down the lower bound for the height.

(b) Write down the upper bound for the base.

7 The temperature is taken as being 21.8°C to one decimal place. What is the least possible actual temperature?

HWK 1E ————————————————— **Main Book Page 250**

1 This rectangle measures 14 cm by 6 cm to the nearest centimetre.

14 cm

6 cm

(a) Write down the least possible length and width of the rectangle.

(b) Work out the least possible area of the painting.

2 A tile weighs 43g, correct to the nearest gram. What is the greatest possible weight of 50 tiles?

3 The distance between two cities is 180 km, to the nearest 10 km. Which range correctly completes the statement below: 'The true distance between the two cities lies between'

A | 170 km and 190 km   B | 175 km and 185 km   C | 179.5 km and 180.5 km

4 Write down the lower bound and upper bound for each quantity shown in the table opposite.

Quantity	Measured as:
weight w	4.16 kg to 2 decimal places
diameter d	81.5 cm to 1 decimal place
mass m	60 g to nearest 10 g
height h	7.36 mm to 2 decimal places
time t	110 s to nearest 10 s

5 A tin of fish weighs 210 g, to the nearest gram. What is the least possible weight of 15 tins?

6

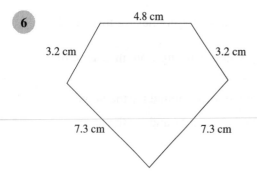

4.8 cm

3.2 cm 3.2 cm

7.3 cm 7.3 cm

Each side of this pentagon has been measured to the nearest 0.1 cm. What is the actual lowest possible value for the perimeter of this pentagon?

7 V = IR is an electrical formula. I = 7.6 to one decimal place. R = 20.5 to one decimal place. Calculate
(a) the least possible value of V.
(b) the greatest possible value of V

8 What is the greatest possible value of A–B if A = 10.8 (to one decimal place) and B = 7.6 (to one decimal place)?

UNIT 6

6.1 Shape and Space Review

Remember:

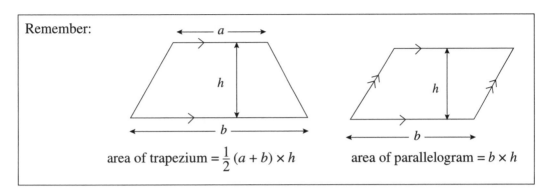

$$\text{area of trapezium} = \frac{1}{2}(a+b) \times h$$

$$\text{area of parallelogram} = b \times h$$

Find the area of each shape. All lengths are in cm.

1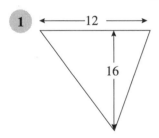

2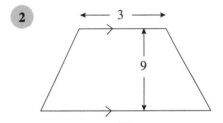

3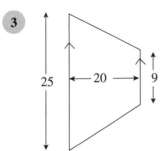

4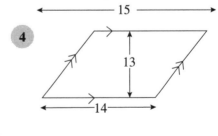

5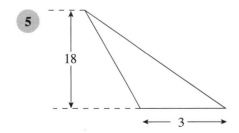

6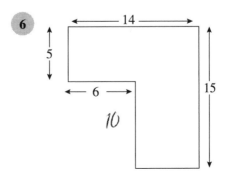

7 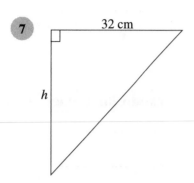 The area of this triangle is 368 cm². Find the value of *h*.

8 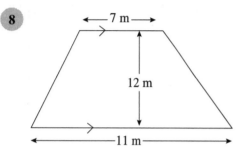 The area of the trapezium is twice the area of the parallelogram. Find the value of *x*.

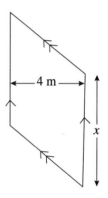

9 Carpet at £18.95 per m² is used to carpet this room.
10% extra carpet is bought to allow for offcuts.
Work out the total cost of the carpet.
(Give your answer to the nearest penny)

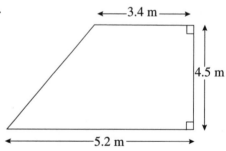

10 Find the shaded area.

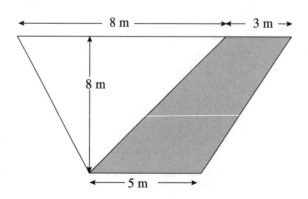

HWK 1E ———————————————————— **Main Book Page 266**

Remember: circumference = π × diameter
area = π × radius × radius

Give each answer correct to 1 decimal place in this Exercise.

1 Find the area of each shape below:

(a)
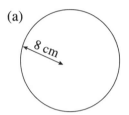
8 cm

(b)
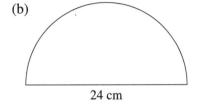
24 cm

(c)
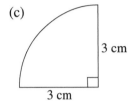
3 cm

3 cm

2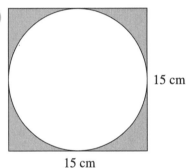
15 cm

15 cm

Find the shaded area.

3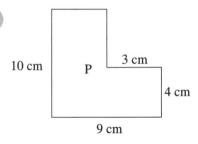
10 cm   P   3 cm
4 cm
9 cm

Which shape has the
longer perimeter and
by how much?

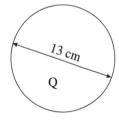
13 cm
Q

4 A bike wheel has diameter 63 cm. How many times does the wheel turn a complete revolution
when the bike travels 25 m?

5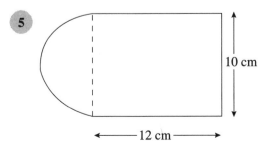
10 cm
12 cm

Calculate the perimeter of this shape.

6 Find the shaded area.

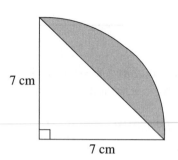

7 cm

7 cm

HWK 2M ———————————————— **Main Book Page 268**

Find the angles marked with letters.

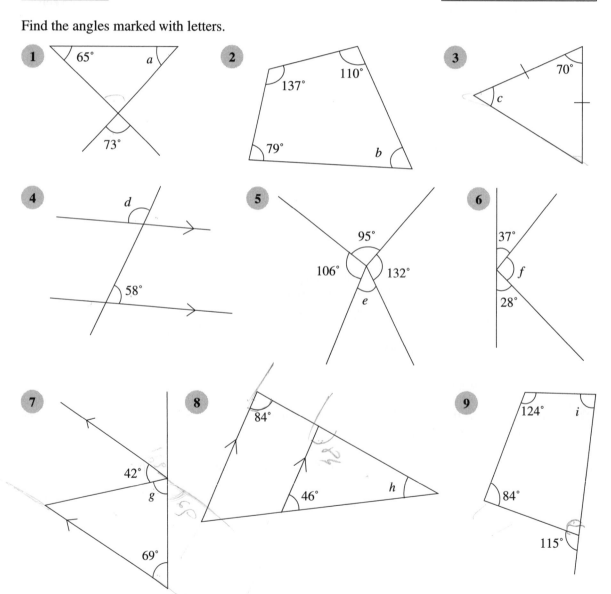

1 65° a 73°

2 110° 137° 79° b

3 70° c

4 d 58°

5 95° 106° 132° e

6 37° f 28°

7 42° g 69°

8 84° 46° h

9 124° i 84° 115°

> Remember: sum of the interior angles of a polygon with n sides is
> $(n-2) \times 180°$

Find the angles marked with letters.

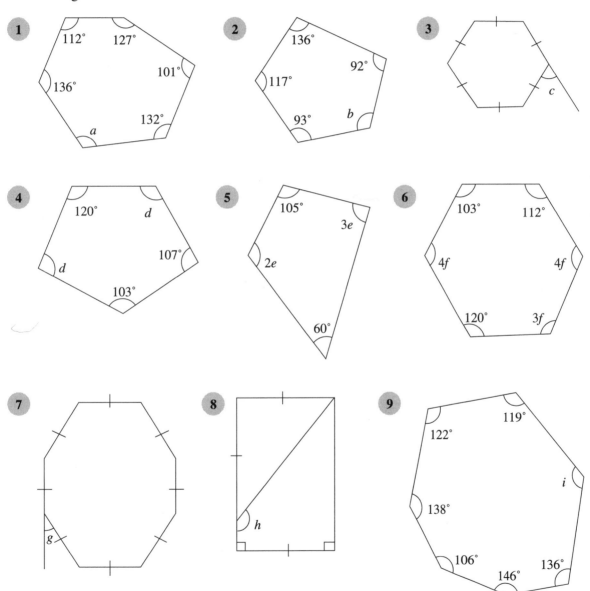

1
112° 127°
101°
136°
132°
a

2
136°
92°
117°
b
93°

3
c

4
120° d
107°
d
103°

5
105°
$3e$
$2e$
60°

6
103° 112°
$4f$ $4f$
120° $3f$

7
g

8
h

9
119°
122°
i
138°
106° 136°
146°

114

You may need tracing paper.

1 Describe fully each of the following transformations.

(a) P → Q

(b) P → R

(c) R → S

(d) S → T

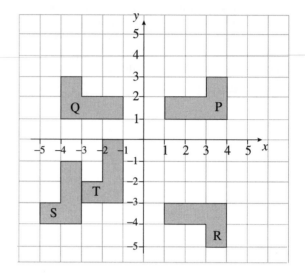

2 (a) Draw x and y-axes from –5 to 5.
Draw a triangle A with vertices at (2, –2), (5, –2) and (2, –3).

(b) Rotate triangle A 90° anticlockwise about (1, –1).
Label the new triangle B.

(c) Reflect triangle B in the y-axis. Label the new triangle C.

(d) Rotate triangle C 90° anticlockwise about the origin. Label the new triangle D.

(e) Describe fully the transformation which maps triangle D onto triangle A.

3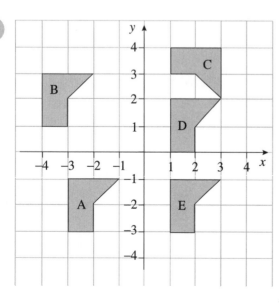

Describe fully each of the following transformations.

(a) A → B

(b) B → C

(c) C → D

(d) D → E

(e) E → A

You may need tracing paper.

1   Copy this shape then enlarge it by a scale factor $\frac{1}{2}$ using the centre of enlargement shown.

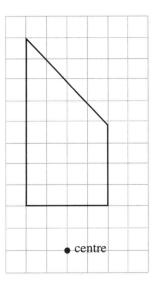

2

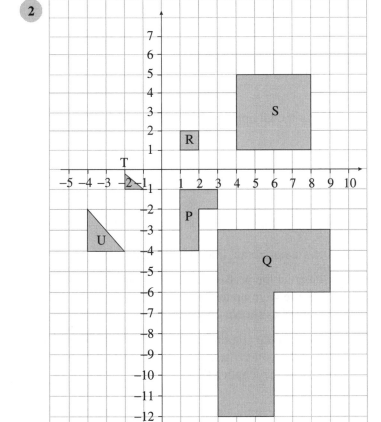

Describe fully each of the following enlargements.

(a) P → Q

(b) R → S

(c) U → T

(d) S → R

116

3 (a) Draw x and y-axes from –8 to 8.
Draw a triangle P with vertices at (–1, 1), (–1, 4) and (–2, 1).
(b) Enlarge triangle P by scale factor 2 about (0, 0).
Label the new triangle Q.
(c) Rotate Q 90° anticlockwise about (0, 0).
Label the new triangle R.
(d) Reflect R in the y-axis. Label the new triangle S.
(e) Enlarge S by scale factor $\frac{1}{2}$ about (0, 0).
Label the new triangle T.
(f) Rotate T 90° anticlockwise about (0, 0).
Label the new triangle U.
(g) Describe fully the transformation which maps triangle U onto triangle P.

| **HWK 4M** | **Main Book Page 272** |

1 Draw a line of 7 cm. Construct the perpendicular bisector of the line.

2 Draw an angle of 50°.
Construct the bisector of the angle.

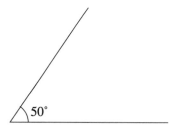

3 Use a ruler and protractor to draw the triangle shown opposite.
Measure the length x.

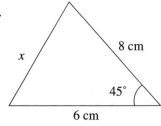

4

N

4 cm

P   M   Q

— 8 cm —

(a) Draw a horizontal line PQ of length 8 cm.

(b) Construct the perpendicular bisector of PQ.
Measure 4 cm up the bisector and mark on
M and N as shown opposite.

(c) Construct the perpendicular bisectors of MQ and MN.
Label the point where these two bisectors meet as X.
Measure the length MX.

5 (a) Use a ruler and compasses only to construct an equilateral triangle of side length 8 cm.
(b) Using this triangle, construct an angle of 30°.

> Remember: a locus is the set of points which fit a certain description.

1 Mark a point A with a cross. Draw the locus of all the points which are exactly 5 cm from A.

2 Copy rectangle PQRS.
Draw the locus of all the points which are inside the rectangle and less than or equal to 4 cm from Q.

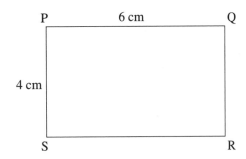

3 S ×

Draw two crosses S and T.
Tina walks so that she is always equidistant from S and T.
Show on your diagram the path that Tina takes.

×
T

4

A ——— 12 m ——— B

6 m

D ——————————— C

Draw this room using a scale of 1 cm for 2 m.
Mark wants to put his TV so that it is 3 m from C and the same distance from wall BC as wall CD.
Show clearly with a cross on your diagram where Mark places his TV.

5 Draw a line PQ of length 7 cm. Draw the locus of all the points which are 2 cm away from the line PQ.

6

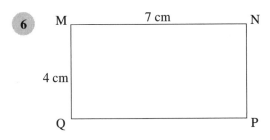

Draw this rectangle. Show all the points which are equidistant from M and N as well as being at least 4 cm from P.

118

Remember:

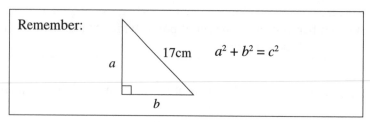

17cm $a^2 + b^2 = c^2$

Give your answers to 2 decimal places where necessary.

1 Find the value of the letter in each diagram.

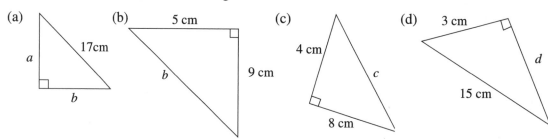

(a)   17cm a b

(b)   5 cm b

(c)   4 cm   9 cm c 8 cm

(d)   3 cm d 15 cm

2

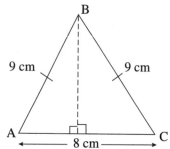

This diagram shows the side of a shed.
Calculate the length of the sloping roof x.

x

3.2 m

2.5 m

2 m

3 Calculate the length x.

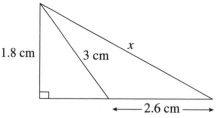

1.8 cm   3 cm x 2.6 cm

4 The bottom of a 4.8 m ladder is 2.2 m from a wall. How far up the wall does the ladder reach?

5 Calculate the area of triangle ABC.

B

9 cm   9 cm

A   8 cm   C

> Remember: volume of a prism = (area of cross section) × length

Give each answer to one decimal place.

1 Find the volume of each prism.

(a)

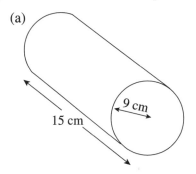

(b)

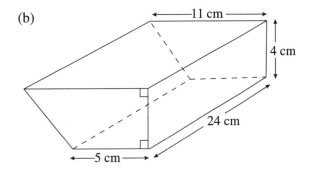

2

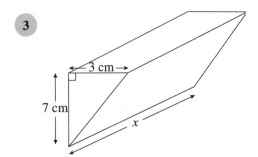

The density of this gold ingot is 19 g/cm³.
Find the mass of this gold ingot.
(Remember: mass = density × volume)

3

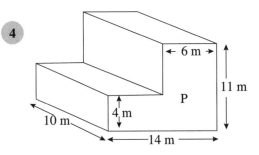

The volume of this prism is 315 cm³.
Find the length x of the prism.

4

Which prism has the
larger volume and
by how much?

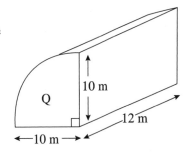

5 This container is completely full of water.
Water leaks out of the bottom of the container
at a rate of 3 cm³/second.
How long does it take before the container is empty?

←—8 cm—→

9 cm

12 cm

6.3 Simultaneous equations

HWK 1M ───────────────────────────────── **Main Book Page 288**

1 Use the graph to solve the simultaneous equations.

(a) $x + y = 4$
   $3x - y = 4$

(b) $x + y = 4$
   $x - y = -2$

(c) $3x - y = 4$
   $x - y = -2$

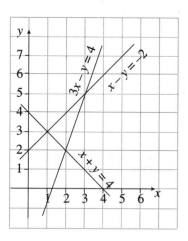

2

Use the graph to solve the
simultaneous equations.

(a) $4x - y = 12$
   $x - 4y = 18$

(b) $3x + 2y = 12$
   $3x + y = 9$

(c) $3x + 2y = 12$
   $x - 4y = 18$

(d) $3x + y = 9$
   $4x - y = 12$

(e) $x - 4y = 18$
   $y = 5x + 5$

Solve these simultaneous equations by drawing straight line graphs first.

1 $x + y = 5$
$y = 2x - 1$

Draw axes with x and y from 0 to 6.

2 $x + 4y = 8$
$2x + y = 9$

Draw axes with x and y from 0 to 9.

3 $2x + 3y = 12$
$3x - y = 7$

Draw the x-axis from 0 to 8 and the y-axis from −7 to 5.

4 $x - 2y = 10$
$3x + 2y = 6$

Draw the x-axis from 0 to 10 and the y-axis from −6 to 4.

Solve the simultaneous equations.

1 $3x + y = 10$
$4x + y = 13$

2 $7x + 2y = 22$
$5x + 2y = 18$

3 $x + 4y = 14$
$x + 3y = 12$

4 $4x + 2y = 26$
$4x - y = 17$

5 $6x + y = 21$
$2x - y = 3$

6 $4x - 2y = 10$
$x + 2y = 0$

7 $3x + y = -1$
$2x + y = 1$

8 $2x + 3y = -1$
$4x - 3y = -29$

9 $x - 5y = 6$
$2x + 5y = -18$

In questions **1** to **3** alter one of the equations and then solve the simultaneous equations.

1 $5x + 3y = 27$
$2x - y = 2$

2 $4x - 2y = 26$
$3x + y = 22$

3 $2x - 4y = -14$
$4x + y = 26$

In questions **4** to **12** alter both equations and then solve the simultaneous equations.

4 $3x + 2y = 16$
$2x + 5y = 29$

5 $2x + 6y = 18$
$5x - 4y = 7$

6 $7x - 3y = -5$
$5x + 4y = 21$

7 $5x + 3y = 46$
$2x + 7y = 30$

8 $7x - 5y = -41$
$4x + 6y = 12$

9 $2x - 3y = -6$
$5x - 2y = -26$

10 $4x - 3y = 33$
$3x + 5y = 3$

11 $9x + 4y = -21$
$5x - 7y = 16$

12 $10x + 9y = -14$
$3x + 7y = 13$

HWK 3E ──────────────────────────────────── **Main Book Page 291**

Form simultaneous equations then find the two unknown numbers in each question.

1 The sum of two numbers is 12. Twice one number subtract the other number is 9. (eg. let the two numbers be x and y)

2 The difference between two numbers is 7. Double one number added to double the other number makes 62.

3 Treble one number added to the other number makes 71. The sum of the numbers is 29.

4 Solve the simultaneous equations

(a) $3x + 2y = 10$
$5x - 4y = 13$

(b) $7x - 4y = 1$
$6x - 5y = 4$

(c) $2x + 4y = 9$
$5x - 8y = 18$

(d) $3x + 7y = 2$
$11x - 5y = -8$

5 A school shop sells folders at £3 each and pens at £4 each. One day the shop sells 19 of these items and receives £70. How many folders were sold and how many pens were sold?

6.5 Inequalities

HWK 1M ──────────────────────────────────── **Main Book Page 300**

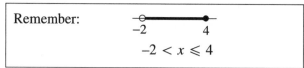

Remember:
$-2 < x \leqslant 4$

1 Answer true or false:

(a) $5 > -6$

(b) $-2 > -5$

(c) $4.2 > 4.16$

(d) $4^2 < 3^3$

(e) $30 \text{ mm} < 4 \text{ cm}$

(f) $2.3 \text{ kg} > 2245\text{g}$

2 Write down the inequalities displayed. Use x for the variable.

(a) ◄────○── 5

(b) ──○──► 2

(c) ●────► -3

(d) ◄────● 4

(e) ○───○ -3   1

(f) ●───○ 0   7

(g) ●───● -6   -1

(h) ○────► 5

(i) ○───● -8   3

3 Draw a number line like those in question **2** to display the following inequalities.

(a) $x \geqslant 3$

(b) $x < -4$

(c) $x \geqslant -1$

(d) $-4 \leqslant x \leqslant 2$

(e) $3 < x < 9$

(f) $-1 < x \leqslant 6$

(g) $x > 0$

(h) $4 \leqslant x < 10$

(i) $-7 < x \leqslant -2$

4 Write a possible number to complete each of the following:

(a) $\boxed{} > 1635$

(b) $-4 \leqslant \boxed{} < -3.9$

(c) $-8 > \boxed{}$

5 Carl's weight w is 76.12 kg. Tanya says that $w \geqslant 76.12$. Is Tanya correct?

6 Write an inequality for each statement.

(a) The minimum percentage, p, for a pass in a maths exam is 45%.

(b) The maximum number of pupils, n, in a class is 31.

(c) A restaurant must average between 15 and 20 customers (c) each evening in order to make enough money.

(d) The greatest height, h, for a child to play on a bouncy castle is 158 cm.

| HWK 1E | Main Book Page 301 |

> Reminder: an integer is a positive or negative whole number or 0.
> eg....., –3, –2, –1, 0, 1, 2, 3, ...

1 Write down all the integer values of n which satisfy the inequalities given below:

(a) $2 \leqslant n < 6$ (b) $-3 < n < 1$ (c) $0 \leqslant n \leqslant 5$

(d) $-5 < n \leqslant 4$ (e) $0 < 3n < 12$ (f) $-6 < 2n \leqslant 0$

2 Write down the smallest integer n such that

$$4n > 39$$

3 Solve the inequalities below:

(a) $x + 4 < 12$ (b) $3x - 1 \geqslant 17$ (c) $5x > 80$

(d) $x - 7 \leqslant -3$ (e) $10 + x < 13$ (f) $x - 4 \geqslant -6$

(g) $7x > 56$ (h) $3y \leqslant 1$ (i) $2x - 1 < 23$

4 Find the range of values of x which satisfy each of the following inequalities and show the answer on a number line.

(a) $6 + x < 11$ (b) $\frac{x}{4} \geqslant 5$ (c) $\frac{x}{2} \leqslant 4$

(d) $3x - 2 \leqslant 10$ (e) $9 + x > 1$ (f) $6x < -30$

124

6.6 Fully functional 3

Go Karting

Three riders, Martin, Helena and Calvin, are involved in a Karting competition.

1 lap of the track is
1600 m long

To change a speed of km/h
into m/s:
    ×1000   then   ÷3600

Task A

From the information given below about the first race, work out the final position of each driver.
The first race is one lap only.

Helena

This graph shows Helena's speed and time throughout the first race.

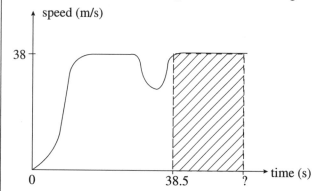

After 38.5s, she travels 608 m
to the end of the race.

Remember:

Calvin

This table shows Calvin's average speed for
each quarter of the first race.

1ˢᵗ	2ⁿᵈ	3ʳᵈ	4ᵗʰ
25 m/s	36.4 m/s	22.2 m/s	33.3 m/s

Remember: use a calculator
with

Martin

Martin's average speed for the whole
race is 104 km/h.

Task B

There are 8 races in total. The winner of each race gets
7 points, 2nd place gets 5 points and 3rd place gets 3 points.
The results of the other seven races are shown below.

M = Martin

H = Helena

C = Calvin

Work out the positions of the three
riders after *all* 8 races.

race	1st	2nd	3rd
2	H	M	C
3	M	C	H
4	C	H	M
5	M	C	H
6	M	C	H
7	H	C	M
8	C	M	H

Task C

The top two riders have a final race to decide on the winner of the competition.

With 100 metres of the race to go, the leader from task B is 6 metres ahead of the second placed rider from task B.

The leader from task B completes the rest of the race at a speed of 36 m/s. The second placed rider from task B completes the rest of the race at a speed of 39 m/s.

Who wins the race? Show all your working out.